CW00342035

GREEN
RACES
RED

GREEN
RACES
RED

EDDIE IRVINE

CollinsWillow
An Imprint of HarperCollins*Publishers*

To my Mum, Dad and grandparents.
Without their support, none of this would
have been possible

First published in 1996 by
CollinsWillow
an imprint of HarperCollins*Publishers*
London

© Tidswell Ltd 1996

1 3 5 7 9 8 6 4 2

The Author asserts the moral right to be
identified as the author of this work

All rights reserved. No part of this publication may be
reproduced, stored in a retrieval system, or transmitted,
in any form or by any means, electronic, mechanical,
photocopying, recording or otherwise, without the
prior written permission of the Publishers

A CIP catalogue record for this book
is available from the British Library

ISBN 0 00 218762 0

Photographs supplied courtesy of
Keith Sutton and Eddie Irvine

Colour origination by Saxon Photolitho, Norwich

Printed in Great Britain by
Caledonian International Book Manufacturing Ltd, Glasgow

Contents

Preface

The chapters that follow tell the story of my first year with Ferrari. But they also look back on my early years in motor racing and touch on the many people who have helped me along the way. I would like to use this book as a means of thanking all the teams for whom I have driven, and everyone who has helped me to get where I am today. There are too many to name individually. They know who they are.

I would also like to thank Jean Todt and the Ferrari team for their assistance and support in producing this book. Thanks also to my publishers, HarperCollins, and to Maurice Hamilton and Keith Sutton for help with the words and pictures respectively. And I must not forget my sister, Sonia, and manager Rod Vickery, for generally keeping an eye on me and helping things run smoothly.

Eddie Irvine
Suzuka, Japan
October 1996

CHAPTER 1

No Big Deal

Ask any young racing driver and he'll tell you that the idea of joining Ferrari means everything. That's the way I felt while racing in Ireland in Formula Ford. It's something to dream about when you're struggling along with few opportunities and even less money. Mention Formula 1 and you automatically think of Ferrari. If a driver gets himself into one of the red cars, he has it made.

But when it actually happens, as it did for me when I joined Ferrari in October 1995, the reality is not so difficult to take on board. The point is, I was not as gobsmacked as I thought I would be.

I don't know whether it's because I get used to things quickly or that maybe other drivers exaggerate when joining a new team. In my case, I never regard anything like that as a big deal. And yet there was no doubt that signing for Ferrari had to be the biggest deal of my life.

I felt much the same at the end of the first race of the 1996 season in Australia. I finished on the podium but, to be honest, third place in the Ferrari was not much to write home about. It meant nothing. For me, it's all about doing a really, really good job – and I didn't feel I had achieved that in Melbourne mainly because the situation was not there to allow me to do a good job.

Anyone could have brought that car home third; the most significant fact was that the F310 had finished at all. It was a minor miracle after the huge dramas we had gone through in the weeks leading up to the start of the season. At one point, after seemingly endless delays and problems, I never thought we would make it to the first race and, if we did, Ferrari would be totally embarrassed.

It just goes to show that you certainly can't take anything for granted in motor racing.

The previous September, for instance, I was absolutely sure I would be spending a third season with the Jordan team in 1996. I didn't really want to do that, but there seemed to be no other way because of a watertight contract with the team.

It's true that team boss Eddie Jordan had given me my chance in Formula 1. He had offered me a drive in the 1993 Japanese Grand Prix at Suzuka and I had taken it. I had spent three years racing in Japan so I knew the circuit well. I had also earned quite a bit of money during my time in the Far East – but Eddie Jordan was not exactly offering a similar reward! It was no big deal in every sense. But I can't deny that it was a good opportunity to establish my name in Formula 1. I managed to do that at Suzuka – although not quite in the way I had expected.

I finished sixth in my first Formula 1 drive and scored a championship point. Everyone seemed pretty excited about that, mainly because Jordan had been having a poor season and, with my team-mate Rubens Barrichello taking fifth place, this was the first time the team had scored any points in almost a year. But as far as I was concerned, the real excitement had yet to come.

During the race, I had been challenging Damon Hill for fourth place. The track was in the process of drying out after a heavy shower, Damon had changed to slick tyres and I was on wets, which were definitely the thing to have while the track was still slippery. I wanted to make the most of my knowledge of Suzuka because I knew where there was grip to be found and I wanted to pass Hill while the going was good from my point of view.

Leader Ayrton Senna came past and lapped me, but then instead of doing the same to Damon he seemed to become over-cautious. Damon's car was sliding around quite a bit and Ayrton was not keen to try and pass. But I was. So I overtook Senna and unlapped myself. It was no big deal … at least, not for me.

It turned out that Senna was mad as hell over that manoeuvre. Nobody had dared to do such a thing to him before. After the race he came down to see me, which was a bit difficult because he wasn't exactly sure what I looked like. He soon found out, however, and we had a discussion, of sorts.

I explained things the way I saw them; I didn't feel there was any need to apologise because I had done nothing wrong. The race stewards had seen no reason to take any action but Senna was not impressed. Apparently I had not shown enough respect. Fair enough; that was his point of view. Case closed.

Except he wanted to leave me a reminder with his fist. The blow knocked me to the floor and onto the front pages of the world's newspapers. Everyone made a meal of the episode but I couldn't see what all the fuss was about. The best bit, I thought, was that Eddie Jordan had missed the drama in his own backyard. Eddie can't resist a microphone or a television camera and, of course, as soon as the news got out, the Jordan garage was inundated. But Eddie wasn't there. He had cleared off on holiday and missed the chance of an important sound-bite or two.

I signed a three-year contract with Jordan at the beginning of 1994 and settled down to learn about Formula 1. Some of the lessons were to be pretty painful. At the first race in Brazil, I became involved in a four-car shunt. I won't go into too much detail now, except to say that the accident had nothing to do with me. Jos Verstappen caused it while trying to overtake as we came across two cars, one of which was in trouble and slowing. Verstappen could see what was going on, and yet he still kept his foot down – even when he went onto the grass. Everyone else was avoiding the accident when Verstappen lost control on the grass, came right into me – and off we all went. It was a huge shunt.

The race officials decided I should take the wrap and I was eventually banned for three races. It was a hell of a penalty. Some time later, there was a bit of back-pedalling by certain people in authority but, at the end of the day, the driver is powerless. There's nothing you can do; you just have to suffer the consequences. That incident really set me back. I missed out on the experience of racing; there is, after all, no substitute for miles behind the wheel. Something like that is bound to affect your confidence, no matter how hard you try to shrug it off.

I spent the rest of the 1994 season learning, picking up points here and there and generally rebuilding my confidence and my reputation. By the time I was half way through 1995, I knew it was time to leave Jordan.

I told Eddie Jordan that, if his team stayed as it was, I would not be driving for him the following year. My wages for 1996 were to be based on the results achieved in 1995. But my car kept breaking down, so on that basis the contract was totally unfair; I had missed out on prize money in 1995 and now it was going to affect my earnings in 1996. Of course, Eddie didn't agree; he said it was normal. There was to be no arguing with him. At that point, I decided to look elsewhere.

At the second race of the season in Argentina, I had met Luca di Montezemolo, the President of Ferrari. I had qualified fourth in Buenos Aires and Luca came to see me. He said 'Well done', or words to that effect. Then he said he heard that I had a Ferrari road car. He had been told that I had tested various sports cars and none of them had been in the same league as my Ferrari GTO. I said that was correct. I had written favourably about it – so perhaps he ought to give me a discount on spare parts! He seemed to like that. I'm still waiting for the discount...

But contact had been made. Not long after, Mike Greasley, who was handling my contractual affairs, spoke to Niki Lauda. The former world champion was acting as advisor to Ferrari and he was interested in finding out about my position with Jordan. My contract had a buy-out clause. When Lauda heard how much Ferrari would have to pay, he said it was ridiculous. So that seemed to be the end of the matter.

After my fruitless discussions with EJ, however, I was taking a serious look around. I talked to Tom Walkinshaw who, at the time, was effectively running the Ligier team. He made Jordan an offer – which was rejected largely because the money was not right and also because a move by me from Jordan to Ligier would be seen as a slap in the face for EJ. He knew people would ask why one of his drivers would want to leave and join a team which was no better. He also knew I would probably tell anyone who asked!

Meanwhile, I had been tipped off to keep in touch with Ferrari. As autumn approached, things began to move quickly. Ferrari were definitely interested in me, but we had to sort out a deal with Jordan. By now I was desperate to leave.

I had been qualifying ahead of my team-mate Rubens Barrichello at most races. There had been a time when Rubens was being hailed as the next Ayrton Senna, but now he was being devalued to the extent that there was no point in me beating him. The guy was no longer in anyone's Top 10. Staying at Jordan was not going to do my reputation any good either; moving to Ferrari had to be right in every respect. If only we could do the deal.

I asked EJ if he could help me go to Ferrari. He said he thought he could – meaning, if the money was right, anything was possible. We flew to the offices of Ferrari's lawyer in Switzerland and agreement was reached. Ferrari had offered a lot of money to have reigning World Champion Michael Schumacher move from Benetton, so there was not much left in the kitty to pay me. In fact, most of it went towards the buy-out clause and into the Jordan bank account. But the most important thing was, I was joining Ferrari.

As soon as the 1995 season ended, my feet hardly seemed to touch the ground. Jordan were extracting their pound of flesh by keeping me busy with public relations work right up to the end of the contract. Meanwhile, I had begun testing for Ferrari.

It was immediately apparent that this was a different world compared to what I had been used to. Ferrari had the resources to get things done. At Jordan, it had more or less been down to my engineer Andrew Green and I to sort things out. At Ferrari, there were people coming at you from all directions. Of course, having the reigning World Champion on board was a big help! They had employed Michael Schumacher because he was the best. Now they had to give him the support he would expect, and I could only benefit from that.

Everyone had been asking me how I expected to cope with being the number 2 to Schumacher. It was if I had committed suicide – they were convinced that my reputation would be totally destroyed by this man – but I honestly could not see the problem. Being the number 2 in the team was to be expected. Schumacher had won the Championship twice and he had put in some rather good performances along the way! Ferrari were going to give me everything they could to enable me to be right behind Michael at the end of each race. Okay, I would not be able to win if I was leading and he was lying second. But that was fair enough. There would be a concentrated effort to win the Championship and Michael had to be a better bet than me. I couldn't see the difficulty with that point of view. Anyway, as the 1996 season approached, the team began to have far more important problems than that.

The new F310 car was late. The deadlines kept being put back, and back, and then back again. Finally, the launch of the F310 was delayed until 15 February, just over two weeks before the car had to be ready for shipment to Australia for the first Grand Prix of the season in Melbourne.

We couldn't wait to get going in the F310. Michael began testing – and ran into problems straight away. Oil was leaking from a spacer which is designed to separate the gearbox from the engine. It was not a simple fix because of the very intricate work in the gearbox itself. Time was running out. It was panic stations; quite unbelievable. Everyone was working their backsides off. I had never experienced anything like it.

With one week to go, we reached the stage where there was no longer any point in panicking; it was a case of simply letting it happen. But, having said that, the team was seriously concerned that we would go to Melbourne and be completely humiliated.

All the spacers kept leaking. We had one remade – and that leaked. It was a gorgeous piece of engineering work, but bloody complicated. Ferrari were the only team to have this spacer, the advantage being that it was very light – provided it worked.

In the end the spacer needed to be redesigned and remanufactured. But that's where Ferrari excel. Because they are so big they can take a chance and, if necessary, they can get things changed. Jordan, for example, could never try and bring a car out that late, because if something went wrong, they would be finished. That's not a criticism. It's just a statement of fact. Jordan could not afford to do something so adventurous, and the very same thing applies to the majority of teams.

Having said that, it seemed very disorganised at Ferrari mainly because we were in so much trouble with so many things. Every time I went to drive the car, something happened. If it wasn't the spacer, then it was something else. We would fix that and then the fault with the spacer would raise its head again. It was problem after problem; quite unreal.

I felt very sorry for the team because the car was beautifully engineered, and extremely well made. It was just incomprehensible that so many things could go wrong. And, as the deadline for the new season approached, life became absolutely frantic.

Ferrari was receiving sponsorship for the first time from Asprey, the jewellers. Naturally, they wanted to make an impact and a very formal function had been arranged for one evening at their premises in London's Bond Street. Michael and I both had to be present. Personally I felt like a bit of a puppet standing around in my bright red driving overalls while everyone else was dressed to kill. Anyway, it was all part of the job, although a much more serious duty was waiting for me at Ferrari's Fiorano test track in Italy.

The original plan (of many!) had been for me to finish final testing at Fiorano, fly to London for the Asprey function and then leave Heathrow the next afternoon for Japan, en route to Australia. Some hope. With everything in such chaos, I was needed in Fiorano the next day.

I got up at 6 am to fly to Milan, and then drove like mad to reach Fiorano because I needed to catch a 2 pm plane from Bologna back to London in order to make the connection with the Tokyo flight. On the way down the autostrada, I rang my engineer to make sure everything was ready. He said, 'Yep, no problem. We're just about to take the car over to the circuit.'

I got to Fiorano, only to find that the car had suddenly developed a fuel leak. Yet another new problem had surfaced from nowhere. These things happen, I suppose. I was told there was no longer any point in me waiting. For once, I was quite happy about the setback; at least I would be able to make a quick return to London. So I set off and, just as I pulled up at Bologna Airport, I received a call from Fiorano with the message: 'Come back'.

The implications were too much to even think about. All week I had been booking flights and changing my plans. My travel agent reached the stage where he did not want to answer the phone because he knew it would be me with another alteration. At one point, I was booked on several flights and I didn't have a clue which one I was going to be able to catch – British Airways, ANA, JAL, you name the flight to Tokyo, and I was on it.

I returned to Fiorano, hopped into the car, drove 200 yards – and there was yet another problem. I had gone beyond the stage of being either surprised or upset. I was almost past caring. The intention had been to go to Tokyo for some meetings and to do a couple of interviews. I could forget that because now I would be leaving London the next day. I just switched off and relaxed. It was a very pleasant afternoon, so I sat in the sun and waited while they worked on the car.

Everything was ready to roll just before dark. We did a couple of runs which were actually quite useful because we discovered something very interesting in connection with the engine temperatures. Once I had finished, I had to see Montezemolo and tell him what the car was like. Then I had to report to Jean Todt, the team manager, and discuss what we had found.

All the while, I was aware that I really needed to catch the last flight out of Milan. I didn't want to leave my departure until the first flight the following morning because the risk of being fogged in at Milan was too great. Either that or not being able to land at Heathrow for the same reason. Travelling between two of the foggiest airports in Europe was leaving too much to chance if I wanted to catch the next flight to Tokyo.

I had not driven the Ferrari flat out during the brief test at Fiorano; that was not the point of the exercise. Certainly, I was far safer in the F310 than I would be during a wild drive to Milan. I have to admit, I drove like a lunatic that night. The little Fiat Coupe I had been given was capable of 140 mph. I was doing all of that – most of it on the hard shoulder! I was overtaking on all sides, absolutely flat out. I just had to catch this flight. It was madness. I was watching the traffic, knowing it would only take some guy in a little Fiat to wander into my path and we'd all be history. I've never been so scared.

I reached Linate airport with five minutes to spare. I stopped at the front door, ran inside the terminal, dumped the car keys at the Alitalia desk and said someone from Ferrari would come and pick up the car on Monday. This was a Friday night! That's the fantastic thing about driving for Ferrari. Once the Italians hear that name, nothing is a problem any more. They rushed me through and I got on the flight by the skin of my teeth.

Despite arriving in Japan a day late, I managed to rearrange my schedule without too much difficulty. It helped that I felt completely at home in Tokyo. I really love going there. Having spent three great years racing in Japan and being based in the capital, each time I return, it seems like I'm reliving my childhood.

All the European or foreign drivers – there was usually about half a dozen of us – would stay in the President Hotel. It was home-from-home and so much more convenient than renting a tiny apartment. Everyone knows me there. I quickly fall into a familiar routine.

I will walk down to the Hard Rock Cafe for lunch, then amuse myself by playing Space Invaders or checking out the latest magazines. Then back to the hotel, perhaps for a snooze before dinner, and then on to the night clubs. I know my way around. I feel very comfortable in Tokyo and, in some ways, it is even better than being in Dublin. It feels more personal. I live near Dublin so I'm obviously in the city quite often. But it's somehow special visiting Tokyo, a bit like returning every now and then to a favourite holiday haunt.

It is an appropriate description because this was the first time I had been able to relax for quite some time. I had arranged to share a flat in Bologna but I had been unable to find time to unwind as the team would regularly call me to Fiorano. It is a forty-minute run on average – I've done it in twenty-three minutes but it's not healthy at that rate. I prefer just to plod along. Inevitably I would show up and a problem would have arisen. I would then return to Bologna, but being on call meant it was impossible to organise anything, and I couldn't even go to the gym. It made life very difficult.

I had to be ready for action at all hours. The team was prepared to run until dark. Sometimes we would go beyond that. There were occasions when it was pitch black but we needed to take the car out, if only to discover what was going to go wrong next. Testing is very spectacular at night because the disc brakes glow bright orange and the row of little lights on the dashboard, indicating when it is time to change gear, flash back and forth. The exhaust pipes spit flames. It's all very dramatic. Fantastic, actually.

It is all part of the atmosphere at Fiorano. The test track, which is owned by Ferrari, is on the edge of Maranello and there is always a sizeable crowd pressed against the fence. As a Ferrari driver, you are continually under the microscope. All the talk among the crowd is about lap times. It doesn't matter that you might be trying various ideas out on the car and lap times are out of the question. In front of the *tifosi*, there is always this pressure to perform.

When I completed my first laps at Fiorano, I was trying to do decent times – and I could tell the team were encouraging that because they kept giving me fresh tyres. With Michael, it was the reverse. They were trying to slow him down because he was a known quantity and they didn't want him to show his hand with the new car.

When Fiorano was built in the early seventies it was way ahead of its time. In fact, Ferrari remains the only team with its own private test facility. It is extremely useful to be able to run the car whenever it suits the team rather than having to book a circuit and then travel to the track in question. Fiorano is so narrow that if you make the slightest error or deviation, it is exaggerated and shows immediately. The *tifosi* will stand there all day. On one occasion, because of problems, we managed just one lap, which was in the dark. And yet the fans waited from dawn to beyond dusk just to see it. There is nowhere else where that sort of thing can happen. It's unreal.

I was thinking about the pressure induced by all that attention while I was flying from Japan to Australia. Tokyo had made the perfect stopping place en route to Melbourne: eleven hours from London then ten hours to Sydney and a short hop from there. It was the perfect split. I had time to reflect on everything that had been going wrong.

I knew it was going to be very difficult for the team but, personally, I was not that concerned. If I am criticised, it usually goes straight over the top of my head. If I'm not doing a proper job, I am aware of it. I don't need someone to tell me. I know when I am wrong and I know when I'm right, and I don't care what anyone else thinks. On the other hand, the Italian temperament is quite soft. They are quite susceptible to criticism and I knew there would be a lot of that flying around in Melbourne.

I really thought the whole Ferrari team was about to be massively embarrassed.

CHAPTER 2

Too Good To Be True

I can sum up the Grand Prix in Australia like this: there were two girls in Melbourne whom I had previously got to know in Tokyo, and we had plans to meet. We spoke on the phone – and that was it. I never did get to see them. From the moment I stepped off the plane, I was flat out from start to finish. That's how difficult it was!

I arrived on Wednesday morning and went straight to a press conference, then on to the circuit where I talked through everything with my engineers. I had dinner in the hotel that night with sporting director Jean Todt, then off to bed. Practice began the following morning, an extra day of testing having been thrown in because the track was new to everyone. Then more lengthy discussions with my engineers, back to the hotel, dinner and bed. This went on without let-up every single day. It was the least fun I had ever had at a Grand Prix! Needless to say, it was a bit of a shock after the more relaxed times at Jordan.

We were in a slightly confused state because the F310 had been reasonably quick from the word go, and yet it felt awful. There was bad oversteer (when the car tries to spin) going into the corners and then, as soon as I touched the throttle, nothing but understeer (when the car tries to plough straight on). And yet the lap times were pretty good. It was all very strange.

Setting-up the suspension and aerodynamics on the car had been a matter of guesswork. Initially I thought the car felt too 'soft', so on the Friday night I asked my engineer to set up the car with a very, very stiff front end. He did that, and the car felt a great deal better. Not perfect, mind you, just better. Since the lap times were reasonable enough, it encouraged the feeling that, if we could sort this car out, then we would be looking really good. As things stood, however, the Williams-Renaults were a second a lap faster. That gave a more immediate indication of our competitiveness.

Everyone was keen to see how I was getting on relative to Schumacher. My lap times had been edging closer to his and, at one point, when we went out together, I was a bit quicker, which was quite nice because I think everyone was expecting me to be blown away by the World Champion.

Overall, I was not as consistent as Michael although I felt I could muster a quick enough lap when it came to qualifying on the Saturday afternoon. I felt reasonably confident. Then an engine failed not long before the end of the final free practice before qualifying. I knew straight away that the time taken to change it would eat into the sixty-minute qualifying session.

The Jordan mechanics could change an engine very quickly – I think thirty-five minutes is the record. It took our guys two hours, which was understandable for a number of reasons. One noticeable difference was that in the Jordan car, the radiator came off with the engine, so whenever a new engine was being prepared, the radiator and engine would go into the car as one. In the F310, by contrast, the radiator is in the chassis, so it has to be disconnected first and the whole system bled.

Everything was new and unfamiliar: the car, the engine, the lot. The net result was that twenty-five minutes of qualifying had gone before I could get back into the car.

In some respects, that was not a total disaster because each driver is limited to twelve laps. But you need time for an exploratory lap before perhaps making some changes to the car to suit the latest conditions. This particular day, in fact, was a classic example. The track temperatures had risen quite a bit since the morning session. As soon as I went out, I suddenly found the car had nothing like the amount of grip that we had enjoyed before. Suddenly I had loads of understeer, and as a consequence we were struggling.

The most immediate answer was to increase the front wing angle and create more downforce. That would give the car more front-end grip and allow it to turn into the corners more easily. It was the correct decision and as a result I immediately went a lot quicker. But it wasn't quite right. And time was running out.

The only thing to do was put on even more front wing and hope for the best. But the trouble was, I only had time to leave the pits and then complete a single fast lap, and that would be it. The way things had been going, everyone had been quickest on their second or third flying laps because it would take until then to get the tyres working really well. I wouldn't have that luxury.

I really tried to work some heat into the rubber by working the tyres hard in the corners during the first lap out of the pits, and I succeeded – up to a point. The front end of the car didn't feel as good as it could have done at the start of the quick lap. But it wasn't bad.

Michael had completed his best lap just as I was leaving the pits. His time was not that quick, to be honest. I thought I was in with a chance, and I knew what I had to do.

From the point of view of timing, each lap is divided into three sections. The split times are thrown up on the computer read-out in the car. I could tell from my time on the first third of the lap that I was three-tenths of a second slower than Michael – which tended to confirm my suspicion that the tyres were not 'in' at that point, that is, not up to optimum working condition. But everything felt better for the final two-thirds of the lap.

My overall lap was good, but not brilliant. It wasn't on the ragged edge. It was a very neat lap, but then the best laps should be neat and tidy. Just as I crossed the line, Luca Baldisserri got on the radio and said, 'Good lap!' They sounded quite happy. I checked the read-out. I was ahead of Michael! But I couldn't tell where I was on the overall list of times.

During qualifying, the officials operate a weigh-bridge at the entrance to the pit lane. Cars are stopped at random and, as I came in, I was pulled over for a mandatory weight check. As I climbed out, everyone was saying, 'Well done! Well done!' It was only then that I discovered I was *third* on the grid!

After all the troubles we had been through, it was hard to take in.

To me, this felt as good as winning pole position. The Williams-Renaults were first and second and we knew they were much faster than anything else. I couldn't help but wonder what I might have done on a second or third flying lap, but I knew there was no way our car was within half a second of the Williams in terms of performance. I was well pleased.

I had to walk the length of the pit lane to get back to the Ferrari garage. On the way, I passed the Jordan pit where everyone came rushing out. There were all sorts of remarks as you might imagine and the one which really grabbed my attention concerned Eddie Jordan. It seemed he had bet Benetton boss Flavio Briatore and Formula 1 supremo Bernie Ecclestone that I would out-qualify Schumacher. Each time that happened, they would pay EJ $20,000. And each time Michael was ahead of me, Eddie had to find $5,000. So, EJ was in front already. I had left the team and he was still making money out of me. I guess it should not have come as a surprise.

There were wide grins when I got back to the Ferrari garage. I couldn't honestly tell how Michael felt; all he said was 'good job', or something like that. This had been the first time in a couple of seasons that his team-mate had been faster than him during a straight fight in qualifying. He had been having his own problems with his car – so he was a bit quiet. Anyway, we were soon into another debrief. With the Ferraris third and fourth on the grid, there was a lot to discuss.

Our strategy for Melbourne was to run the quickest race that we could. That may sound an obvious thing to say but there were variables to consider, particularly concerning the number of pit stops. It was clear that Williams would be on a different level to us, whereas I thought that the Benettons (sixth and seventh on the grid) were probably not as quick. It would be a case, as I said, of choosing the right tactic to suit us. There was no point in trying to out-guess Williams; they could do whatever they liked – one, two or three stops – and still win the race. The computer worked out that a two-stop race was best for Ferrari, so we settled on that.

In my opinion, there had been a lot of rubbish talked about pit stop strategy in 1995. It was said that Benetton were smarter than anyone else. I don't think that had much to do with their success. Michael Schumacher, who was with Benetton then, was simply quicker than the rest of us. He could carry more fuel than the Williams drivers and still run with them. Then, because he already had more fuel on board, he needed to take on less at the first stop and he was able to get ahead by doing that. It was simply down to Michael being quicker than anyone else. The so-called experts talked about Benetton's strategy being a lot better but the simple fact is, if you are not quick, then you are not going to win.

Back to the present and sitting on the second row of the starting grid, I wasn't under any illusions about winning this race. In any case, there was a minor distraction when something was dropped on the front wing of my car as we sat on the starting grid. It meant changing the whole front wing. During the reconnaissance lap on my way to the grid, I had found that the car was understeering too much and I had asked to have more wing angle added at the front. This had been done but I don't think the replacement wing had the same setting.

The 1996 season really got under way when the red lights went out – they had done away with the green lights in a new starting procedure – and I watched the Williams drivers, Hill and Villeneuve, make a race of it off the line. Damon Hill got himself into a bit of a mess at the first corner, the Williams going sideways. I remember thinking, 'Damon is too easy' because I saw a bit of a gap and went for it knowing that Damon wouldn't close it. In fact, he had screwed up so much that he actually let Michael through as well. I thought this was pretty good. Jacques Villeneuve was leading, I was second and I knew there was no way Damon would get past Michael until the first pit stops at the very earliest. It was a great way to start.

Then the red flags came out. The race had been stopped, which was a big disappointment considering I had made such a good start. I didn't know the exact reason but I assumed there had been an accident somewhere during the first lap. We returned slowly to the starting grid and somewhere along the way I saw pictures of what had happened. Going into the third corner Martin Brundle, who had started from the back of the grid, had piled into a couple of cars which seemed to be involved in their own accident. A chain reaction had been caused by one car moving over on another, which in turn forced David Coulthard to take avoiding action. The McLaren, which may in turn have been touched from behind, swerved into Johnny Herbert's Sauber just as Brundle arrived on the scene. Brundle hit Herbert and became airborne and rolled a couple of times. It was a big shunt. Martin was lucky because of the way the car had bounced. He was unhurt, but it was ironic that he was driving a Jordan.

There had been a bit of controversy over the way Jordan and Williams had interpreted new rules concerning the introduction of raised cockpit sides in order to give more protection to the driver's head. Jordan had been a bit cheeky by bending the rule in such a way that they did not need to raise the cockpit sides as much as everyone else. There was a performance advantage to be had by doing that. It may have been very small but that was not the point. This was all about safety and I felt that Jordan's decision to do what they did was totally wrong.

Formula 1 does not need people getting smart when it comes to safety. On this occasion, Jordan were extremely lucky. Martin's head could have gone over the side of the cockpit. They were fortunate because of the way the car rolled and the fact that there were no G-forces and no heavy impacts with the concrete wall.

The car had broken in half immediately, the engine coming away from the chassis, which meant there was not a huge amount of weight adding to the car's momentum as it continued to roll. It was the 'perfect' sort of accident – if you can say such a thing – one which looked highly spectacular but, in fact, did not amount to a great deal.

Had Martin suffered a serious impact to his head, then I would hate to think what the newspapers would have done with the story in the light of some of the comments which other team owners had been coming out with regarding Jordan's interpretation of the cockpit rules.

Ron Dennis, the boss of McLaren, was reported in *Motoring News* to have said (before the accident) that car designers, because of the loophole in the regulations, had to ask themselves a serious question: 'Are you going to make your car deliberately less safe to achieve a performance advantage, even if that advantage is improved lateral vision?'

Can you imagine what the tabloids would have done with that had Brundle received a serious head injury?

At the end of the day, it was the responsibility of the FIA technical delegates and they had passed the Jordan as legal. The fact remained, however, that the designers of the Formula 1 teams had drawn up the rule. What had become clear was that two of the designers knew they were going to find an advantage with the very rule which they were helping to establish. The sport's governing body had asked the designers for their help. It was totally wrong for two of them to then use a loophole.

Anyway, the main thing was that Martin was perfectly okay. That's the first concern when you see another driver have an accident; you just hope he gets out. When he does, you then shut the whole thing from your mind.

I have to admit, that was much easier to do than usual because of my position near the front of the grid. When you are in the middle, it's a nightmare. When you are at the front, you've got the two guys ahead, and that's it. Once I had seen Villeneuve and Hill get going, I could take a quick look behind to see who was there, and then get on with the business. Further back, however, it is much more difficult to register exactly what is happening. The basic rule of thumb is that the driver following has to watch the guy in front and try to work out what he is going to do. In effect, you look after your front wheels. That's the law as I see it.

At the restart in Melbourne, once again I made a better getaway than Damon but this time he got through the corner without making a mess of it. The Ferrari was definitely lacking in acceleration and straight line speed. Whether it was a question of insufficient power or perhaps too much aerodynamic drag, I'm not sure. All I know is that I was on the clean side of the grid (in effect, on the racing line which had more rubber and less dust and dirt) and twice I beat Hill off the line, and twice he left me way behind.

While waiting on the grid, I had been thinking about trying to get rid of the understeer. I didn't want to make too many adjustments as this would take me further away from the original set-up arrived at during practice. It would have been a risk to make further changes because the understeer could have been caused by the tyres not having enough temperature at such an early stage of the race. In the end, we left the car as it was. Maybe, with hindsight, we should have done a bit more because, as soon as the race started, I knew I was still in trouble.

After the first couple of laps, I felt there was no point in trying to push as the understeer would destroy my front tyres. I had to apply caution and simply try and maintain my position.

With Villeneuve and Hill in front that meant I was third, with Michael closing on me. We had agreed before the race that, if I was quicker than him, then he would move out of the way and vice versa. It made good sense. The deal was that I could run my own race if I was faster than Michael, but, if we came to the last corner and I was third with Michael fourth, then I would let him through. I had no problem with that. Michael was employed to win the Championship. As far as I was concerned, it would be three points instead of four. Big deal. Who needs statistics?

We had agreed that if Michael felt he could go quicker than me, he would radio the pits and then my engineer would speak to me and just say 'Michael'. That would be the signal and I would let him through. Since I was struggling with understeer and Michael was closing on me, it was pretty obvious what was going to happen. But I wanted to allow him though without letting the Benetton of Jean Alesi get by as well.

I chose the back straight, a place where Alesi might not expect such a move to take place and, even if he did try to come through, there were a couple of twisty corners immediately afterwards which would help me keep him at bay. The trouble was, I think I caught Michael by surprise as well! He ducked out from behind me at the last minute but luckily it worked out. Alesi missed his chance.

I knew I couldn't run with Michael; I was just too slow. Whether that was because of the understeer, or whether he was just quicker than me, I don't know. Interestingly, in the morning warm-up (when we run in race trim in final preparation for the Grand Prix) the two of us had been separated by just a few hundredths of a second, which was quite satisfying.

In any case, I was also concerned about brake-wear during the race. I knew from experience that I tended to be a lot harder on the brakes during the race than I had been when qualifying. We had measured my wear-rate on the Ferrari and, if the usual percentage increase occurred, I would have great difficult finishing the race. But this was speculation because I had not had the chance to put in a full race distance during testing with Ferrari, so we didn't know how big the problem might be. I had no choice but to take it easy. To be honest, even if I had pushed hard, I could not have run with Michael. My race was with Alesi and the Benetton. I just tried to be smooth and not make any mistakes. Unfortunately, with Alesi, you never knew what was in his mind.

Approaching the braking area for a very slow corner – one where I was troubled by the understeer – I took a look in my mirror. I saw Alesi give some thought to coming down the inside, but he was too far behind. I reckoned there was no chance of him coming through from that distance, so I didn't worry about him.

Then I looked again and there he was, on a mission to nowhere. In fact, he lost control of the Benetton before he even hit me. The impact could have been a lot worse; he could have spun me out of the race. In fact, the Benetton damaged part of my rear wing so I took things easy during the next few laps, just to check that everything was okay.

It was typical Alesi. He seemed to get away with that sort of thing at almost every race. Going into the first corner, not long after the start of the previous year's Belgian Grand Prix, he came barrelling down the inside with his brakes locked up. I was ahead of him and, if I had turned in to the corner – which was totally my right – he would have gone into the side of my Jordan and the race probably would have been stopped. And I know who would have been blamed. In the event, I gave him room and lost several places in the process. This time, however, he paid for his impatience.

It was great, because Alesi's retirement took the pressure off me for the rest of the race. I was able to drive at my own pace; in fact, I was able to pick up speed because I could smooth everything out and drive neatly without having to play a defensive game. I found about two or three tenths of a second per lap and, by no longer needing to worry about braking that little bit later just to stop Alesi from coming through, I was removing the worry about brake wear.

The rest of the race was uneventful. I moved up to third when Michael dropped out with mechanical trouble, but I was not pushing at all. I was thinking: 'I've got to finish, I've got to finish. I can't believe this is happening.'

This, of course, was the furthest I had gone in the new car. That's when you learn things – such as the fact that I was moving around a bit too much in the seat. It seemed a snug fit when I tried it for the first time, but, after an extended period in the cockpit, I was making mental notes about where I needed extra support. I was learning about the way the car was handling, which was very useful experience for the future.

It was quite funny because it occurred to me that, if the Williams drivers crashed into each other, then I would win! I would be like Nigel Mansell, who won his first race for Ferrari in 1989, against all odds. Nigel had been in an identical situation, as the new Ferrari had been plagued with problems. They were introducing a semi-automatic gearbox and Mansell was lucky if he managed a handful of laps during practice without the car coming to a halt. The warm-up for the race had been a shambles. I believe Nigel had booked himself an early flight home. He really didn't believe he would finish the race, never mind win it. When he did, Italy went beserk.

I was thinking: 'That would be great if the same happened to me!' But then I thought about the Australian Grand Prix at the end of 1995. I was holding an easy third place and thinking what a great way this would be to leave Jordan. Then the engine failed.

That made me feel worse. Each lap seemed to get longer and longer. By the time I got to the end of lap 58, I was delighted to see the chequered flag. Everyone at Ferrari was even happier.

I was pleased for the team as much as anyone else because they had worked so hard. But, to be honest, I thought the best thing I had done all weekend was to qualify third; that had allowed me to stay ahead of trouble in the race. Anyone could have come home third under those circumstances. It was no big deal. But at least it justified a beer or two afterwards. Then I had to jump on a plane back to Europe at midnight. And I never did get to see the two girls.

CHAPTER 3

Showing My Colours

The buzz I felt after finishing third in Australia had nothing to do with the result. Michael had been waiting for me in parc ferme. I think he said: 'Good race, well done.' It was difficult for me to hear exactly because my ears were ringing.

Most drivers use ear plugs while in the car to cut out the engine noise; they also double up as speakers for the radio system. Unfortunately, mine had fallen out during the race. The team had been trying to tell me to speed up because Jacques Villeneuve was in trouble, but the message wasn't getting through. I could hear a buzzing in my ears every now and again. I knew my engineer was trying to say something but I assumed I had a problem of some sort, so I was going slower and slower – and the more I backed off, the more I was being told to speed up!

After the race, people were talking to me, but I couldn't hear them clearly. My ear plugs had never fallen out before. It must have happened gradually, because I didn't notice them go. I was just increasingly aware of the engine; in the end, the noise was unreal. I had noticed other drivers taping the plugs into their ears before the start of the races; I made a point of doing that from then on.

Meanwhile, there had been a noise of a different kind following events on the rostrum in Melbourne. The usual arrangement at the end of a race is for the first three finishers to take their place on the podium and the flags of their respective countries raised behind them, the winner having his national anthem played at the same time. In my case, they put up the Irish flag because I race under an

Irish licence, more as a matter of convenience than a political statement. The Irish flag is green, white and orange and it was designed for the whole of Ireland; green for the Republic, orange for Northern Ireland with white for peace between the two. The problem is, the so-called Tricolour has unfortunate connotations in Northern Ireland because it is seen to soley represent the Republic. People in the North have been told for as long as I can remember that the colours are green, white and gold. I had only discovered the proper meaning a year or so ago; it made me wonder if this green, white and gold business had been deliberate misinformation by those who want the Union Flag flown in Northern Ireland.

Anyway, I was not about to get into Irish politics when the officials asked me, before the Australian race, which flag I would prefer: the Irish or the British. I said I didn't mind. To be honest, I didn't really care because I was sure I wasn't going to finish. Ideally, I would have liked a flag with a shamrock; something with no political overtones. The officials had also asked about the national anthem if I won. I thought that was pushing my luck a bit too far but, just in case, I had asked for the 'Londonderry Air', a traditional tune which everyone knows, very Irish but completely non-political.

I suddenly remembered all of that when I was on the rostrum. I looked behind me but, from where I stood, I couldn't make out which flag they were using. Unfortunately, a number of people back home could see the Irish Tricolour all too clearly on television.

My Dad received several telephone calls; there were letters of objection in the Northern Ireland newspapers; all that sort of thing. I had raised the subject with the sport's governing body, the Federation Internationale de l'Automobile (FIA). They said it was either the Union Flag or the Irish Tricolour. They didn't appreciate the delicate situation and they didn't want to know about anything else. So, we had the Irish flag in Australia and, all of a sudden, attitudes softened a few weeks later. I don't know why; maybe someone at the FIA had a phone call or a letter and the full implication of the Irish question was brought home. Someone said the Irish take these things very seriously. Tell me about it!

I was born and brought up in County Down, Northern Ireland.

The best part of my education came from Regent House, a very good school in the market town of Newtownards, about ten miles from Belfast. The majority of boys at Regent House were Protestant and I can remember the day when a teacher asked if we wanted a united Ireland. I had never understood the politics or the economics of the situation; I just thought: 'It's *one* island, it should be *one* country. Yes, we should have a united Ireland. Why not?' I can't remember the exact numbers but quite a few pupils held the same view, which was surprising considering, as I said, this happened to be a largely Protestant school.

It made sense then, and it makes sense now. If you live in Northern Ireland and you are not Irish, then what are you? Saying you are British is not the answer. The front of the 'British' passport says 'The United Kingdom of Great Britain and Northern Ireland'. Strictly speaking, people from the north of Ireland are part of the UK. A number say they are British and hold allegiance to The Queen but – and this is just my personal opinion – The Queen is only a figure head, someone who mainly attracts tourists. And you have to say that she does not bring many visitors to Northern Ireland. I agree with having a Queen but I think the rest of the Royal family and the hangers-on are nothing more than a total waste of money.

I would class myself as Irish in the same way that David Coulthard says he is Scottish. A Scotsman doesn't necessarily say he's British even though, in the strictest sense, he has more right to make that claim than someone from Northern Ireland.

Obviously there has been a lot of talk over the years about Northern Ireland losing its links with Great Britain. I've heard it said in the North that the people from the South want to come along and take over Northern Ireland because it's 'a great little country with a great little economy'.

They must be joking. Northern Ireland is a wonderful place but, when you look at the infrastructure, you can see there's not a lot going for it. The main industries are heavily subsidised by the British government; we produce very little off our own bat that is financially viable in a big way. If Northern Ireland lost its links with Britain, it would be an economic disaster. The Republic of Ireland has a forward thinking, young government. But it couldn't cope with the financial burden which would come with the North if we were to have a totally united Ireland. There has got to be some sort of compromise and I'm sure one could be worked out if intelligent, logical people were allowed to get on with it.

In my opinion the younger generation, North and South, are not really bothered about this old fashioned dogma about keeping the two sides apart. I am convinced that if there was better cross-border transport communication – a much-improved train or bus service, for instance – then the flow back and forth would help to heal the divide. Young people are not into the politics. They simply want to live their lives on both sides of the border and better communications would help them do that and strengthen the bond as a matter of course. I should stress that this is a personal opinion, although I would like to think that I am not alone in my views.

The trouble is, people on both sides of the border are hamstrung by minorities living in the past. I find the Reverend Ian Paisley a total embarrassment, a man who has set the Unionist cause back a hundred years. When we went to Argentina for the Grand Prix, I was with some friends when the television news showed Orangemen (Protestants) having a punch-up in Belfast. They wanted to walk down a certain road and the police wouldn't let them because it would inflame the situation in a sensitive area where Catholics lived. They were shouting and screaming, intent on causing aggravation on the pretext that they had walked down the road for donkey's years, so why should they change now. My friends wanted to know what the trouble was all about. I said: 'Don't even ask, it's just too difficult to explain. You wouldn't believe it possible of grown men.'

I have to admit I was put on a bit of a spot when I came into Formula 1 and certain assumptions were made about the orange and green on my crash helmet. I had started out with a plain white helmet but I was advised early in my career to make it more distinctive. I chose orange because it stood out. Okay, it was a coincidence that there was the orange connection with Northern Ireland, but there was no political statement involved whatsoever. If the Orangemen's colour had been purple, there would not have been purple on the helmet. I wanted a bright colour. Yellow had been taken by someone else. So I chose orange.

The original markings along the side made the helmet looked similar to Ayrton Senna's; it was assumed I was modelling myself on him. In fact, the shade of orange I used at first made the helmet look yellow in photographs. I changed it to a richer shade of orange and then added the green stripes, just to make a point about the Irish connection and the orange not being a political statement.

I have to admit I played on it a bit when asked. I would make comments about the religious divisions in Northern Ireland and journalists didn't know how to take it. This is obviously a serious subject and they weren't sure whether or not I was joking; they didn't want to case offence over a matter which, sadly, is life and death for some people on both sides of the Irish border.

The fact is that I that I haven't been to church since I was old enough to avoid going to Sunday School. And I have no intention of going to church now because, in Ireland, religion creates so much aggravation. My parents and my grandparents were not churchgoers even though, in Northern Ireland, the majority of the community attended church. The numbers have dropped in recent years but, even so, church attendance in Northern Ireland remains much higher than in most parts of the United Kingdom.

I don't have strong feelings either way. I think you are either good or you are bad. I don't know which is right and which is wrong. There may be a lot of people who are right but, on the other hand, there seems to be a tremendous number who are wrong. Who's to say which is correct? Is it right to say that anyone living in the jungle, because of their lack of knowledge of religion as we know it, will automatically go to hell? What kind of logic is that? But then, the way things have been with the situation in Northern Ireland during the past twenty-five years, it's not for me to talk about logic!

I was actually acting a bit stupid myself during the few days I had off between the Australian Grand Prix and the next race in Brazil. I decided to have a go at sorting out the back garden of my house in Dublin. I went at it like a bull in a china shop and ended up hurting my shoulder, which was a silly thing to do.

My house is in Dalkey, a very nice area just south of Dublin. The garden covers about half an acre and the guy who had the house before me cut down a number of trees in order to improve the view across Killiney Bay. I was to discover that he had trouble with the neighbours; the police had been called in to try and stop him and I only wish they had succeeded. I would prefer to look at trees rather than the water; I can walk to the bottom of the garden any time I feel like a view of the Irish Sea. Now, after this man's over-enthusiasm with a saw, the garden had been left in a right mess. There were bits of tree everywhere. I had to chop them up and drag them out of the garden. I like doing that sort of thing; it makes you feel as if you are achieving something instead of going round in circles all your life.

I don't want to create the impression that I like manicured lawns and neat gardens; quite the opposite, in fact. Given the choice, I would prefer a forest. I like to let it grow and forget about it. But, before I could leave the place to its own devices, I had to drag the felled trees out of the way. That's when I hurt my shoulder; as a result, I wasn't particularly looking forward to the overnight flight to South America.

In fact, it was great. British Airways had seats in First Class which folded into beds. I find it very difficult to sleep on my back but this meant I was able to lie on my front. It was fantastic. I didn't have dinner on the flight; just a small snack, which I much prefer. Then, head down, off to sleep, no problem at all. I woke up with half an hour to go before landing in Brazil. It was living in the lap of luxury; a complete contrast to what greets you on arrival in Sao Paulo.

It amazes me how the Brazilians can be such happy people while living under such terrible conditions. Looking at it logically, if you weren't an optimistic, easy-going person, you couldn't live the way they do. I like Brazilians; they're good fun. But I certainly don't like Sao Paulo. The river that runs alongside the road from the airport is a rich brown colour. It's probably not as bad as it looks because there are birds catching fish, so the water must be able to support life. But I wouldn't like to go for a swim in it.

I don't feel comfortable being in Brazil. When you think about the money people earn from Grand Prix racing, it is put in perspective when you see the way so many hundreds of thousands have to live Sao Paulo. It causes a conflict of emotions. I hate seeing things like that; on the other hand, maybe it's better that we are aware of such poverty. It makes me think about the attitude of certain people in Northern Ireland who are unemployed and believe they're hard done by. A few minutes spent in Sao Paulo would alter their outlook.

Typically, of course, the problems of the world are soon left behind when you climb into a Formula 1 car. Nothing else matters and I would have plenty to hold my attention within minutes of practice starting.

For the first time, I had one of the latest steering wheels fitted to my car. It does everything. Apart from carrying the paddles which we use for the clutch and to change gear, there are buttons for the radio, as well as for scrolling the read-out, operating the pit lane speed-limiter and selecting neutral, and there are dials for adjusting controls such as the brake balance. Across the top of the wheel is the digital read-out, which gives lap times and other information, as well as the display of sequential lights, previously mounted on the dashboard, which signal the moment to change gear. Using the wheel to actually steer the car is almost incidental.

I drove out of the pits and I couldn't believe how hard the wheel felt. It was like holding a vibrator – not that I've ever handled such a thing, of course! These were vibrations from the engine. Whenever I reached 16,000 rpm, there were 16,000 vibrations per minute going through my hands. I had never experienced anything like it and I felt sure there must have been an engine problem of some sort. I went through the first two corners and then down the straight. As I went into the third corner, a left-hander, I was just about to radio the pits to tell them about the vibration when – bang! – the rear of the car hit a bump and I was off the road and into the barrier. Just like that. I couldn't believe it.

The car had turned sharp left and spun onto the inside of the corner; normally, when travelling at speed, the car would be thrown to the outside of the corner. In this instance, I was going so slowly, the car shot straight across the grass on the inside and removed most of one side – wheels, suspension, radiator – against the barrier.

I didn't know what to think. It was one of those things. There was no alternative but to walk away. I was given a lift back to the pits with Sid Watkins, the FIA doctor. It looked as if it had been quite a big accident and he checked me over. There was nothing wrong with me – which was more than could be said for the car. It wouldn't be fixed until after practice had finished, so that was it for Friday. Half a lap and no progress whatsoever.

Nobody in the team said anything because they could see from the telemetry that I hadn't been going quickly. It was an easy corner, so it shouldn't have been a problem. There wasn't much grip on the track at that stage and the tyres were probably not up to temperature. Even so, it came as a big shock.

I was really worried about the following day. By the time I got started on Saturday morning, everyone else would have done thirty laps, so they would have been much better prepared. However, within four laps, I had set a competitive time, so I knew it was not a major problem.

I qualified in tenth place, which wasn't too bad considering the alterations that had been made to the car because of the problems we had experienced in Australia. The gearbox had been changed to an older specification because the new one kept cracking and the casing was in need of a redesign. This had a knock-on effect because the return to the 1995 gearbox meant we also needed to go back to the old floor. I don't know whether it was these alterations which made a difference to the handling of the car in Brazil, but it certainly did not feel brilliant.

The Interlagos circuit is run anti-clockwise and is a strange one; people who succeed in Brazil for some reason don't do well anywhere else, and vice versa. I had not been helped by discovering that my car had sprung a fuel leak moments before qualifying was due to begin. I had to jump into the spare car, which didn't have the latest differential and that made a big difference in slow corners.

I was very cautious during my first qualifying run and yet I was only one tenth of a second off Michael's time at that stage. But my position on the grid gradually fell as others improved. I went out with another set of tyres and found a bit more time, which surprised me because I didn't feel I had gone that much faster and yet it was a much better lap than the first one. I could only assume that the track conditions had improved.

I went out for a third time and Mika Hakkinen in the McLaren deliberately held me up by backing off in the middle of a fast right-hander, so I had to go off line. I could forget that lap. I waited for Hakkinen – if he thought he was being smart, then I could be smart as well – and I held him up on the start of his attack lap.

I had one lap left. I pushed really hard but, on the last corner, the back of the car stepped out of line and that cost three-tenths of a second – which made a big difference. Michael was on the second row and I was on the fifth row. There may have been just half a second between us, but it was night and day.

I couldn't complain because I was in the spare car, I didn't have the right set-up, and I had made a mistake. But that didn't get away from the fact that I was tenth on the grid, which, on paper anyway, didn't look that good.

We spent a lot of time discussing everything in great detail and I didn't get back to the hotel until early evening. James Bowles, a friend with whom I occasionally stay when I am in Oxford, had come to Brazil. I left specific instructions with the front desk to let James into my room. He arrived at 8 am and, at 7 pm, he was still sitting outside the hotel because they wouldn't let him into my room. He was not happy!

Having James there made life a bit more fun than it had been in Australia. Unlike Melbourne, where the teams were in various hotels scattered across the city, everyone uses the Hotel Transamerica in Sao Paulo, mainly because it is comfortable and close to the track. It is a sociable place as a result; quite lively at night. Once again, I didn't go out much in the evenings. The local speciality seems to be the Churrascaria, a popular type of restaurant where they serve as much meat as you can eat. They carve it off massive swords, straight onto your plate. Maybe once in a while is okay, but eating slabs and slabs of meat can't be good for you. It didn't appeal to me, so I usually ate in the hotel.

When I woke on race morning, I had a feeling that the day wasn't going to work out. In fact, the feeling had persisted all weekend. Even before I went to Brazil, I was telling people not to bet on a good result at Interlagos. So far, I had been proved correct and I didn't feel it was going to get any better.

The warm-up wasn't bad – but neither was it good. The car felt okay, nothing more. I told myself not to take any chances in the race, just plod round, bring the car home and perhaps score a couple of points. Then, just as we were about to go the grid, the heavens opened. It really poured, the track was flooded and the car was aquaplaning. I was thinking: 'You don't want to be tenth on the grid in these conditions.' Just for good measure, the engine began to misfire and they couldn't do much about it at that stage.

I made a good start initially but then found I couldn't control the throttle because I didn't know how much power I was going to have at any given moment because of the misfire. People started to go past me as we went onto the straight in a cloud of spray.

I was really scared. I just couldn't see a thing. I couldn't see beside me, nor could I see in front or behind. When it's like that, you just drive, hoping that you are going fast enough to avoid having someone go into the back of you, but not so fast that you are going to drive into the back of someone else.

Racing in wet weather is the most dangerous aspect of Formula 1. The worst place here on the Interlagos circuit was at the end of the long straight. Damon Hill was leading and, if he had spun in the middle of the track, no-one would have been able to see him. We would have cannoned into each other; it would have been carnage.

You think to yourself: 'It's time they did something about this.' But the problem is, the officials are not sitting where we are. They are up high in every sense of the expression. They can see the cars, so they assume we can too. But if they checked the pictures from the in-car cameras, they would soon be aware just how dangerous it is. Nothing ever seems to be done until there's a big problem. It was complete madness in Brazil and everyone was extremely lucky that nothing serious happened.

I was dropping back because of the misfire, but then the spray began to clear. I was really struggling just to stay on the track; the car didn't seem to have any grip. I was running a one-stop strategy because that would give us better options to stay out longer if it looked like the track might dry. In fact, we came in three or four laps too soon because we thought the rain was going to continue. I had another set of wet tyres and no sooner had I rejoined than it stopped raining and the sun came out. That meant losing 45–50 seconds coming back in for slicks. The track was drying but we had a lot of downforce on the car in order to cope with what we anticipated would be a wet track. That meant I was very slow in the dry.

I was so embarrassed. Ferrari were doing badly and I was wondering what people were thinking. I tried to push, but as soon as I did that, the car would understeer and I'd be off the dry line, onto the wet line and I'd lose a lot of time. The last thing I needed this weekend was another trip onto the grass and into the crash barrier. It was one of those races where you would look a complete idiot if you spun off. Quite a few drivers had left the road. But I could not afford to be one of them.

It was only when the track had dried across most of its width that I could actually push hard enough to allow the car to drift out. I set my fastest laps near the end of the race, but they were a second and a half off the pace. That was unreal; absolutely unbelievable.

Damon Hill won his second race in succession for Williams. I came home in seventh place, very disappointed. But the team seemed happy enough. Michael had finished third. He did a bloody good job to get the car home in that position. Starting at the front had helped a huge amount, of course. But he was not very happy. He had been lapped and no one could remember the last time that had happened, if ever, to Michael Schumacher. The only consolation for me was that my fastest race lap was only two-tenths of a second slower than Michael's best.

It was just as well, perhaps, that we were not in a hurry to leave the following day. I had a lie-in before sitting quietly by the pool and mulling over what had gone wrong during the weekend. I was a bit pissed off, to be honest. Melbourne had removed a lot of the pressure. Now it was back on again. What flag did I want on the rostrum, indeed. I should be so lucky.

CHAPTER 4

A Couple of Points

Not many people know this, but I was almost called Stirling Moss Irvine. My father, Edmund, was a massive fan of motor sport. I remember seeing a picture of Stirling Moss after he had won a race – I think it was in North America, at Watkins Glen or Mosport – and there's my Dad standing beside him with an arm around his shoulders. He was quite serious about naming me after his hero. You can hear it now: 'Stirl Irv.' My mother stopped him, thank God!

It was only natural that Dad and I should go to the races together. We regularly went to Kirkistown, our local circuit about twenty minutes away on the Ards Peninsula, and we would make frequent trips 'across the water' to Ingliston in Scotland and Croft in County Durham. The highlight each year would be the British Grand Prix; our summer holiday would revolve around that. We would visit my cousins in Durham and go ice skating, and then motor down to either Silverstone or Brands Hatch.

I much preferred going to Silverstone because it was harder to sneak into Brands Hatch! I have never paid to get into a Grand Prix. One year, my cousin and I were caught digging a hole under a fence at Brands Hatch. Two policemen told us to move on but, when they walked off before we did, we took that as meaning we had full permission to proceed!

Our family ran a scrapyard and Dad would buy and sell cars. I remember one time he took in a Ford Capri and had it resprayed. I cleaned it and when I had finished, this car looked like new, it really did. It was worth £800 and we swapped it for a Crossle 32F single-seater. It was a brilliant deal for us because the guy wanted £1,400 for the Crossle. That was a reasonable price for a 32F. Suddenly, we had a racing car in return for a Ford Capri.

The previous owner had only done a couple of races in the Crossle. He had put in new brake pads just before the start of the second race, got to the first corner – and went straight on. The radiator was damaged, but very little else.

I had a driving license as soon as I reached seventeen. I drove the Crossle a few times but, before I had the chance to race it, we switched to a 50F. This car, which was newer than the 32F, looked a lot better, but it was actually a load of rubbish. I went slower in the 50F than in the 32F. It may have been a very good deal, but to be honest it wasn't the best career move.

Mondiale, a company based in Bangor, my local town, had brought out new cars for the 1984 season. Wealthy Irish businessmen were either driving or running these Formula Fords. There was a major championship meeting at Mondello Park, near Dublin, and I qualified fourth or fifth, ahead of all the Mondiales and just behind the Irish Champion. So Mondiale approached me and said they would like to do a special deal!

The plan was to use my engine, gearbox and other bits and pieces, and they would supply the chassis. I put my new car on pole for the next race but Alan McGarrity, a local driver, and I had an accident at the first corner. I went to the next race, won pole position again and led all but two laps. McGarrity had been punting me up the backside every time I braked. Eventually he got past me and I finished second. I would have liked to have won but, I must admit, I was pleased with the result. At that stage, I had no thoughts about going into motor racing full time. It was out of the question because we had no money. I was racing purely for fun – or the 'crack', as they say in Ireland.

When I left school, I had started dismantling cars in the scrapyard. On a Sunday, the place would be closed, but I would go in and mess about with starter motors. If three didn't work, I would make one good one out of the three. It was my business in effect because I looked upon it as my Dad's 'factory'. I really enjoyed it.

I worked hard when I was there. My grandfather, who was still involved with the business at the time, said I was the best worker in the place. He would try to wind me up, but I was just as bad as him and I knew what he was doing. Unfortunately my cousin Stephen, who also worked in the yard, took Grandad too seriously and allowed himself to be wound up very easily. Grandad would be giving Stephen a hard time – telling him he was a lazy so-and-so – and winking at me at the same time.

It was good fun, except in the winter when it tended to be very cold and wet. You could bet it would be a day like that when someone would ask for a starter motor from a car which was under four or five other cars. I would have to get the crane and lift everything off.

I worked with Stephen and a friend, Derek, who lived down the road. The crack was great. When stacking cars we would save time by having Derek, who hooked up the cars, take a lift across on the crane's hook rather than climb down one pile of cars and then clamber up the other. I remember walking down the road one day with a couple of friends and seeing Derek swinging above the rooftops. It was a big crane and Stephen had Derek hanging onto the hook. He was being swung from side to side and then Stephen would lower the jib, but not before jamming on the brake and jerking the line. If Derek had fallen off, he would have broken his neck. But we were laughing our heads off at the time.

The procedure in the scrapyard was that all the good bits would be removed from the car. Then we would throw in some old tyres and put a match to them. You wouldn't get away with that now. It was like the oil fires in Kuwait at the time of the Gulf War. We would wait until the wind was blowing away from the neighbouring clothes lines, and up she would go. Sometimes the wind would turn. But once tyres start burning, you can't put them out. The neighbours would be up in arms.

Then my job would be to crush what was left – but I had to be careful. Grandad would rip all the copper wire out of the cars once they had been burned, but he made a habit of not saying when he was coming in to work! I was up in the crane one day when I caught sight of Grandad's dog running round the outside of a car I was about to crush with a three-ton weight. He was inside, doing his bit by removing the copper wire…

There was a very good market for the bits and pieces we removed but, even so, we didn't have enough spare cash to go motor racing properly. The most we ever spent in a year was £7,000. Mondiale put forward a deal for me to race in England with Murray Taylor, a New Zealander and former journalist who ran a team. Mondiale asked for £7,000 on the understanding that they would pay the rest. My father and I thought this was the way to go.

Dad arranged an overdraft and paid the money. I finished third in my first event and everything was fine for about three or four races. But then I started slipping back. Reflecting on it now, the Mondiale just wasn't good enough and the engines were poor. The chassis probably wasn't stiff enough and that affected the engine. I'm pretty sure that's what caused the drop-off in performance; the chassis loads up the engine, which means the engine can't work.

It is a terrible feeling knowing that you are going to a race and the car isn't going to be competitive, no matter what you do. It doesn't matter if it is a Formula Ford or a Ferrari. I was to be reminded of that struggle when I went to Argentina for the third round of the 1996 World Championship.

The only way to remember the weekend in Buenos Aires is to talk about the two points I collected for finishing fifth. Everything else was a bit of a disaster – starting with qualifying. The car was awful. It was badly affected by the bumps on the track and wouldn't turn in to the corners. I didn't know what the F310 was going to do next because it depended on whether I hit the bump with the front or the rear of the car. It was on a knife-edge all the time. I was to discover that such problems do not seem to affect Michael Schumacher as much as everyone else, and that didn't make me feel any better.

I had been really looking forward to racing in Buenos Aires. I like the city; it's a brilliant place, really beautiful. The girls are perhaps not as pretty as everyone claims, but they definitely have a certain something. They're very attractive, and they add to the warmth generated by a city which is very cosmopolitan; 'Italians who speak Spanish and think they're British' was one interesting interpretation which is probably quite close to the truth.

On the Wednesday evening, a few of us were invited to President Menem's residence. He had some lovely paintings from artists no one had heard of, but they were very nice works of art. I thought Carlos Menem was a bit of a cool dude. His daughter is a 'babe', very warm and happy, quite laid back. We had pizza and Coke, which was a nice way to do it; very informal and relaxed. President Menem is a motor racing nut. He's been there and done it; he knows what he is talking about. His daughter is the same, and they've both got a sense of humour, unlike most politicians and dignitaries you meet.

Michael was there, as were people from Shell and Marlboro who support the Ferrari team. There were a number of Argentinian businessmen present and one of them was the country's biggest wine exporter. He said he had an agent in Oxford and promised to send me samples of their best wine. I said I would be only too pleased to do my bit for Argentinian exports. In fact, by the time practice and qualifying had finished three days later, I was ready for a bottle of something pretty potent.

The Buenos Aires autodrome is a circuit I like; I had qualified fourth for the previous year's Grand Prix. But now, because of all the problems associated with the Ferrari, I was afraid of the car. I was almost scared to turn the wheel.

That's the difference between a good car and a bad car, it doesn't matter what Formula we are talking about. When you can arrive at a corner and just turn in without any worries, that's when the car is good. That's when you do respectable lap times. If you can't do that, then you haven't got a good car. End of story. I could see the difference between myself and Damon Hill and Jacques Villeneuve in the Williams-Renaults. They could turn into the corners with confidence because the Williams was very predictable. It has a roll-on effect because that sort of thing makes you think you are on top of the job and driving well.

It's amazing the difference it can make. For example, you could be driving all day during a test at somewhere like Snetterton in Norfolk and the car isn't as you like it. You think you are driving like a plonker and you wonder if it's you or the car. Then you make one change to the set-up and go half a second faster almost immediately. All of a sudden you are driving well. You think you are good again, and the car is doing all the work.

The only positive thing to be said was that Argentina was the sort of circuit where you could probably get away, to a lesser degree, with having such difficulties because there were no high speed corners which would really highlight the problem. Even so, it was so difficult to drive that I couldn't see where I could pick up any more time; I just couldn't go quicker.

I qualified in tenth place. I was a bit annoyed because I had been held up during my fast lap and we could tell from the read-out that my predicted time for that lap would have been worth sixth or seventh place. I had Coulthard ahead of me and he pulled out of the way to let me through. Damon, who was immediately in front of David, didn't see me and he was slowing in order to try and get a clear piece of road ready for a quick lap. I was briefly trapped between the two cars and that was enough to screw up the lap. It was a bit of a shame, but these things happen.

Michael had qualified alongside Hill on the front row. You could understand why he gets paid so much money. He's on the pace every time, whether the car is good, bad or indifferent. He has the 'Senna Factor'; in other words, even if the car is bad, he can drag it onto the front of the grid. They can make changes to the car and, okay, Michael may say it feels better as a result. But, at the end of the day, it doesn't matter what the car is like, he will simply find the lap time from within himself. That was very evident in Buenos Aires.

From my point of view, things seemed to go from bad to worse during the warm up on race morning. I did a lap and then the car broke down. It was an engine-related problem and I had no option but to park by the side of the track and watch everyone do their thing. We had made some changes to the set-up: softer on the rear springs to try and make the car more forgiving on the entry to a corner; more front wing in order to try and help the front of the car turn in to the corner.

Not having had an opportunity to try the changes during the warm-up, I managed a couple of laps before going to the starting grid. The car suddenly felt much better. It was the first time such a thing had happened at this stage in a race weekend. Usually, the car felt at its best with less fuel on board. This time, it actually felt better with more fuel. I approached the race feeling a lot more confident than I had before.

I made a good start. At the second corner, I was trying to go round the outside of Villeneuve when he moved me wide and put me onto the grass. To be honest, I would have done exactly the same thing had I been Jacques! Heinz-Harald Frentzen passed me as a result; then I got back in front of the Sauber again. And that was it. Stalemate. I was stuck there.

Barrichello, running in seventh place, was holding everyone up and it became clear that the only way positions were going to change was through different refuelling strategies and faster pit stops.

For instance, I was holding ninth place and running right behind Mika Hakkinen when he pulled into the pits to refuel. Since I was not due to stop for another eight laps, he had been running with less fuel than me, so the Ferrari was therefore quicker. I knew that, if I could push hard for the next few laps, I would eventually get ahead of the McLaren once my first stop had been made. I caught Barrichello quite quickly but, unfortunately, he was on a one-stop tactic, which explained why he was so slow. That, in effect, wrecked my plan because, with overtaking being next to impossible on this circuit, my pace was being dictated by the slow Jordan. Realising that I was going nowhere, the team told me to come in for my first stop – which turned out to be a bit slow – and I rejoined behind Frentzen. I was going backwards!

Then came another twist just before half distance when the Safety Car suddenly appeared and the field had to form up behind it. A car had overturned and the marshals needed to work on it in safety. Just as they were about to sort that out, there was another emergency when a Ligier, which had just made a pit stop, caught fire in a big way and spun off.

The driver, Pedro Diniz, was lucky to escape with burns to one hand but I thought *The Sun* produced the headline of the year when the following day's paper had the words 'Diniz In The Oven' above a picture of the Brazilian sitting in his blazing car. Otherwise, this affair was certainly no joke.

A refuelling valve on the side of the car had not shut properly and the Ligier was brim full of fuel. It doesn't need much fuel to spill onto the hot car before you have a big blaze. I had been through a similar experience when my Jordan caught fire during the previous year's Belgian Grand Prix.

I really can't see what refuelling adds to a Grand Prix; if anything, it screws up the racing. The whole thing has become too complex with teams trying to work out their strategy, while outguessing everyone else. The spectators haven't a clue what's happening; it's just plain stupid.

This is supposed to be Grand Prix racing. We should fill up the cars and go for it. That way, there is more skill involved because the driver has to look after his tyres while running with a full load of fuel; he has to think about that aspect much more. He's actually got to overtake the guy in front rather than rely on pit stop tactics. Granted, he might be able to overtake during a tyre stop, but the chances of that happening are less, which is as it should be. Motor racing is not about overtaking in the pits.

But, having said all that, the most serious problem with refuelling is the threat of fire. The sport is dangerous enough, without having that extra risk. I would like to see a referendum carried out among the informed people in Formula 1. I know what the answer would be. And so, I suspect, do the people in charge. Just ask any mechanic who has to stand there, waiting for a red hot car to come into the pits with up to 100 litres of fuel under pressure just behind his shoulder. Refuelling has its place at Le Mans; it's necessary, a genuine part of endurance racing. But it seems totally false in Formula 1.

As I said, Diniz was lucky. And it was fortunate that the accident happened while the Safety Car was already out on the track. It meant we were stacked up behind the official car for three of four laps and, during that time, my water temperature rose to a critical point, something which would play a part later in the race.

It is the luck of the draw when the Safety Car appears. In this instance, it worked in Barrichello's favour because he was able to make his single stop and lose very little ground while the Safety Car was out. The rest of us, meanwhile, knew we would have to make a second stop once the race was under way.

When the Safety Car pulled off, I got behind Frentzen and dummied to go down the inside of the Sauber. He pulled across to block me – and lost control at the braking point for the next corner. Round he went and into the gravel. I was pretty pleased with that! Once the final pit stop had been made, I chased after Coulthard and harried him for the next few laps. Eventually he made a mistake and I nipped into fifth place. I knew I could take it easy during the final ten laps. Jos Verstappen was sixth in the Arrows but, even though he was closing, there was no way he could catch me. Or so I thought.

With four corners to go on the last lap, my car became stuck in sixth gear. It seemed as if I had actually stopped, because whenever I braked, the engine just went 'blauggghhh' . I thought, 'Oh shit! That's it. Four corners from home and two points gone.' I was gutted after such a good race; I had really enjoyed it after the trials and tribulations of practice and qualifying.

Verstappen caught me very quickly. I was pulling at the paddle on the steering wheel, desperately trying to select a lower gear. The problem was that the exhaust had broken and that, in turn, had overheated the part which makes the transmission change gear. It was seizing up. Eventually, I got it to change down through the gears.

Verstappen came alongside me – and outbraked himself! He ran wide, and I pushed the Arrows even wider to help him on his way. In reality, I didn't really need to do that because he had got himself into a lot of trouble. He had screwed up so badly, that he dropped right back. I don't know what he did exactly, but I was able to take off in first gear and head towards the line.

Now I was stuck in low gear, waiting for Verstappen to come blasting past. But he never appeared. I made it to the flag in fifth place and, two corners after the finish, the car stopped completely. I was really pleased to get two points out of an eventful race which hadn't promised much.

CHAPTER 5

Formula Ford and Fray Bentos

I was told I would never make a racing driver for as long as Murray Taylor had full use of his lower orifice. Except that Murray, being a fairly blunt Kiwi, didn't say it that way. I saw Murray when we were in Melbourne for the Grand Prix and he still seemed fairly normal to me – or as normal as he is ever likely to be – so on the basis of his inaccurate prediction about my future it was perhaps no surprise that his racing team in the UK closed down not long after I had become a professional racing driver.

At the time, however, I was on the dole. I became one of Maggie's Millions after Murray had taken my Dad's borrowed £7,000, given me a handful of races and then fired me. As far as I was concerned, I had done nothing wrong. The problem, as I have already mentioned, was that I just wasn't quick in the Mondiale. Neither was my team-mate, Tony Walsh. He had won the Marlboro Challenge competition which was designed to take promising drivers off the street and make them racers. Tony's prize was this Formula Ford drive, even though he had never driven a racing car before. Looking back on it now, I probably screwed up his career. Everybody thought I was no good and therefore the same applied to Tony because he was even slower. In fact, he was only two or three-tenths of a second away from my lap times which, in his first year, was probably pretty good. But, because I was considered to be a bit of a dead loss, then Tony was thought to be an even bigger one!

I had only managed about seven events, which worked out at around £1,000 per race. My father could have sued, but I really didn't want to get into the politics of the whole thing. We had a contract with Murray Taylor, but I think he spent too much money on the wrong things. He was trying to run his operation like a big-time works team, and Mondiale didn't have the money to support that. Murray put too much emphasis on aesthetics. He admired Ron Dennis and the way he had gone about making McLaren what it is today; it seemed to me that Murray was trying to copy Ron – which is not what you need to do in Formula Ford. When you are working on a limited budget, the emphasis is on making sure the car is mechanically sound and then sending it out. Don't worry about painting it. Just go racing.

A small racing car manufacturer called Quest gave me a couple of races later that year and I didn't like their car at all. I thought it was twitchy as hell. This was only my third season. During the first year, I had taken part in just seven races; in the second year I did eleven, which meant I had no experience at all when I arrived in England and jumped in the deep end with Taylor. In Ireland, the cars tended to be set up very soft. The Quest was stiff and very nervous; I just couldn't drive it. But it was a useful experience. The guys at Quest were really good, a lot of fun to be with. It was very decent of them to give me the drive because I never paid them; I couldn't find any money.

As I said, I was unemployed and, to be honest, I was not in a hurry to find a job. The benefit payments meant something like £18 or £19 in my hand. I had been used to living off the £15 a week earned while working for my father; I even managed to save money from that. It was no surprise, therefore, to find that I couldn't spend £19 a week, not even after I had paid the rent. That was an unusual arrangement at the time because I was living with a nurse in a hostel in Stevenage. She was Tony Walsh's cousin and, strictly speaking, I wasn't supposed to be in the nurses' home at all. It was actually a den of iniquity; I discovered that nurses are, shall we say, quite wild!

At least that made up for the lack of success on the race track. I wasn't sure if I should be thinking about making a career out of racing or simply living day by day. I have to say that it wasn't much fun at that stage and things seemed to get worse when I rented a house at Weedon in Northamptonshire.

I stayed in bed for most of the time; at one point, I did not step outside for four days. The lounge in the house had a plant which looked as if it had died some time before. It was supported by a cane. This was in the days before remote controls for television. I would lie on the sofa and use the cane – which had a metal piece attached to one end – to adjust the controls on the television. I didn't have to move. Talk about high technology.

I was told that Weedon is famous for the invention of radar. Eighty years ago, apparently, birds which looked as though they had been microwaved used to fall out of the sky over Weedon after they had run into the radar beams. Our problem was a danger of freezing to death. I was sharing the house with Mark Goddard, another would-be racing driver, and we couldn't afford to run the heating. It was so *cold*. Mark knew somebody who worked at the Fray Bentos factory and we ate that stuff every single day. Mark didn't take to the pies, but he liked the puddings. It was the other way round for me, so I ate all the pies and Mark ate all the puddings...

I managed to raise a bit of cash by buying a road car for myself and then selling it on. I loved the thrill of making money on a good deal! I eventually raised £4,500 to buy a year old Van Diemen Formula Ford. Auriga, the tuning company, let me have an engine at no cost, on the understanding that I paid for the rebuilds.

I had not even sat in the car when I went to Brands Hatch and qualified in tenth place for a race on the Grand Prix circuit, which I had never been round before. This was all new to me because the race was a round of the 1986 RAC Championship (the leading Formula Ford series in Britain) and I had not competed at this level. Once the race had started, I worked my way up to third place. I was absolutely flying. I had caught the leaders when the race was stopped because of an accident. At the restart, I had to go back to the position I had been in on the previous lap, which meant dropping to fifth. That was no problem because, before the stop, I had just set the fastest lap of the race. I overtook the fourth and third-place guys once more and I was thinking how easy it was.

Then I crashed at Paddock Bend, the quick, downhill corner at the end of the main straight. That was that. But I was pretty impressed.

So, to a certain extent, was Ralph Firman, the owner of Van Diemen. It wasn't good for business to have someone in an old model go quicker than the most recent Van Diemen, so he offered to fit a new front suspension to my car!

I finished fourth at Thruxton and then moved on to the next round of the RAC Championship at Silverstone. I can't remember exactly where I qualified but I do recall running in an easy third place behind Jason Elliott and Phil Andrews, the leading lights of the series. By my standards, these guys were earning mega-bucks in works equipment – and I was sitting right on their tails in a second-hand car.

Everything was under control until near the end of the race. A young guy from Austria was two cars behind me but he tried to snatch third place in one go. Halfway through Copse Corner he came charging over the kerb, flew into the side of me and spun us both out of the race. The doctor ran over and asked if I was okay. When I said I was, he asked if my head was all right. I said: 'It's not *my* head you should be worried about. You should be looking at that tosser over there!'

That was my first encounter with Roland Ratzenberger and our careers would follow similar paths until poor 'Ratzy' was killed during that terrible weekend when Ayrton Senna had his fatal accident at Imola in 1994.

Despite that incident with Roland, this had been good for my confidence. It was the best I had managed since taking part in the Formula Ford Festival for the first time in 1984. The Festival is the big thrash at the end of the season; everyone goes for broke and the driver who wins it is remembered over the winter. The entry is usually so large that they need several heats and, if you reach the final, then you are up against the very best. I remember reaching the final and finishing seventh, the highest placed Irish driver. I had been very pleased with that.

Coming across from Ireland, the tendency is to think that the English and the foreign drivers are superstars. So, to finish seventh from an entry of 160 was a great feeling. The following year, 1985, an Irishman by the name of Hector Lester lent me his Formula Ford

Mondiale for the festival and I put it on pole for my heat. I got as far as the quarter-final, where I hit another guy who had spun off on oil. But to dump what was a fairly old car on pole for my heat – 49.4 seconds, I remember the time very clearly – was a special feeling too. The results with the Van Diemen in the rounds of the RAC Championship in 1986 were the next best thing. I felt I was beginning to get somewhere.

Then, all of a sudden, I started being massively off the pace. I was finishing outside the top six, not figuring in the battles at the front. I had done so well and I had no idea why this was happening. A guy called Malcolm Pullen – known as 'Puddy' – was the chief mechanic at Van Diemen. He had been very good to me and he had offered to help out with some second-hand bits and pieces if I needed them. Puddy could see that I was really struggling – I was something like a second and a half off the pace – and he offered to set up the car for me if I brought it to a race at Snetterton, which is where Van Diemen is based.

I wasn't a very good mechanic and I gladly accepted Puddy's offer. I was so bad, in fact, that the Van Diemen must have been massively underweight by this stage because I hadn't bothered to replace anything which had fallen off! For instance, when Ratzenberger drove into the side of me, I simply threw away the damaged panel and carried on. Other bits of broken fibreglass had never been replaced. I was not very well organised, to say the least.

I had a helper, Philip, who was my cousin Stephen's younger brother, and he came with me to Snetterton in the lorry that we used to carry the car. When we came to unload the Van Diemen, Philip thought I had a hold of the car, and vice versa. The thing just rolled off the top and – boof! – crashed about six feet onto the ground. We looked around. No-one had seen it happen. So that was all right!

I had put the battery for the Van Diemen on a charge overnight in the kitchen – and then left the battery behind. I had also forgotten my crash helmet! It would be a case of begging and borrowing. A few years before, I had lent my helmet to a Formula Ford racer called Perry McCarthy; it hadn't been a problem because we were competing in different races. At Snetterton, Perry was in the

Formula 3 race, so I asked if I could borrow his helmet. He said: 'No. I've only got the one.' I thought: 'Thanks very much!' Perry had finally landed a big sponsorship deal that year and he was a bit carried away with himself. He will probably be surprised that I have remembered the incident but I never forget things like that. Anyway, I try not to talk to him now that I am in Formula 1 and he is still struggling to do something with his career!

Martin Donnelly, a Belfast man who was very quick and would make it into Formula 1 before having his driving career wrecked by a massive accident during practice for the 1990 Spanish Grand Prix, lent me his helmet. He may as well not have bothered. Once again, I was hopelessly off the pace.

The only thing I want to remember about that race was a brilliant overtaking manoeuvre when I ran round the outside of Gary Ayles, a leading runner, going into the Esses. I had the car completely sideways while braking, full opposite lock all the way with one of my front wheels inside Gary's front and rear. Even though Ayles blasted past me on the straight, I think that was one of the best overtaking manoeuvres I have ever pulled. That was the great thing about Formula Ford; you could get away with moves like that. You can't throw around a Formula 1 car; it suddenly snaps out of line and you are immediately out of control. There is no fun in that.

Generally, though, there was no pleasure to be had from driving my Van Diemen. Puddy agreed that there was something seriously wrong with my car and he took a look. We thought he had found the problem. I had renewed two big bolts which held on parts of the rear suspension to the gearbox. Unfortunately, I had been given the wrong size bolts (they were for a later model Van Diemen) and I had tightened them as far as they would go. The trouble was, the bolts were not actually doing anything and the rear suspension was flexing as if it was made of rubber. So, having found the problem, or so we thought, the correct bolts were fitted and I returned to Snetterton – and went no quicker! It was still a mystery and, in fact, it would be another year before I would discover the source of the problem. By then, I would be the works driver for Van Diemen.

Ralph Firman had been trying to get Paul Warwick (brother of the then Grand Prix driver, Derek Warwick) to drive the Van Diemen Formula Ford but Paul wanted to take the next step up to Formula Ford 2000. Puddy was pushing very hard for me, as was John Upritchard, Van Diemen's sales manager who happened to come from Belfast. I had more or less agreed a deal with Ralph, but nothing had been signed. He wanted me to test the car at Snetterton, just to see how I compared with Ratzenberger, who had just won the 1986 Festival. When he saw my time was faster than Ratzenberger's, Ralph was finally convinced. He immediately said 'sign here' and told me to come up with the money, which I think was about £12,000. I had made about £5,000 from buying and selling cars and I gave that to Ralph. He did not pressured me for the rest because, during 1987, we were flying. I had the best car. I said that if I didn't win the championship under those circumstances, then I would go back to Ireland.

Sure enough, I walked the RAC Championship and, even though that meant having to miss one or two rounds of the Esso Championship, I scored enough wins to collect that title as well. It was a fantastic year. The only problem I encountered came about three or four races from the end of the season. Just like the year before, I suddenly found I was off the pace for no good reason. I couldn't understand it.

The car was handling well but I just wasn't quick enough. At one point, I hopped into my team-mate's car and, immediately, I was back up to speed. Then I returned to my car, and could not repeat the lap time. We changed the gearbox on my car. It made no difference. We changed the engine three times in one day and, each time I went out, the lap times were exactly the same: 1 minute 9.9 seconds. I remember it distinctly. Whatever we did, it was 1 minute 9.9 seconds, about one second off the pace.

Then we changed the chassis. At the next race, I was on pole by about half a second and I won the race. I went to the Formula Ford Festival and won that easily. The new chassis was obviously the answer. The original chassis had started to flex through wear and tear and it was immediately obvious that this had been the cause of my problems the previous year. It was the only explanation.

I was lucky. That sort of thing can ruin a driver's career without him knowing. People who buy old cars are often beaten before they start. If anyone asks about running a second-hand racing car, I tell them to get a new chassis before they even think about spending money on anything else. Do that and the car will be as good as new. Overlook the chassis and you will be banging your head against a brick wall. As it was, however, I was sitting on top of the wall at the end of 1987. I was the man to beat in Formula Ford. I wouldn't be going back to Ireland after all!

In fact, I was going to be quite busy, even during the off-season. There was a so-called Winter Series for Formula Ford 2000. These are advanced Formula Ford cars with slick tyres and wings and Ralph asked if I would like to drive the works car in the Winter Series at Brands Hatch. I said: 'No problem'. Come to think of it now, things had been going so well that I should have asked for a wage!

I won a couple of races and, going into the final round, I was up against Jonathan Bancroft in a Reynard. In order to become champion, I had to win. He was on pole and, since it was dry, I knew the Van Diemen could not beat the Reynard. I made the best start and edged over on Bancroft a little. He wouldn't give way. I clipped the Reynard and Bancroft went into the barrier. I won the race.

Bancroft put a protest in and the officials threw me out as a result of video evidence. They had no right to do that because video evidence had not been available at the other races so, according to the rules, it was not admissible in this instance. There had not been any reports from the official observers at the scene so, strictly speaking, there was no evidence. I agree, it had been my fault even though I had been far enough in front of Bancroft for him to make a decision and get out of the way. I was intimidating him, but that is a common tactic under those circumstances at Brands Hatch. As a result, I lost that championship and I thought I had more than reasonable grounds on which to protest. I was persuaded not to.

John Webb, who ran everything at Brands Hatch, suggested to Ralph Firman that I should forget about the protest. At that time of year, the Grovewood Awards (or the Cellnet Awards, as they had been renamed) were presented to promising young drivers.

Right: I always find time to play. At home with my sister Sonia (right).

Left: The biggest boat I've ever owned. So far.

Right: As a youngster I look quite bored while waiting for my father to take to the track at Kirkistown.

Left: Scooping the swimming awards at an early age (that's me, front row, second right).

Right: Hardly Armani. Posing as a teenager with the Crossle 50F at Kirkistown.

Left: Racing in the family. Dad puts his Lotus 18 through its paces at Kirkistown.

Below: The man to beat in 1987. Pressing on in the works Van Diemen.

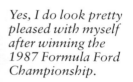

Yes, I do look pretty pleased with myself after winning the 1987 Formula Ford Championship.

Leading the Formula 3 field in 1988.

With James Hunt and his girlfriend, Helen Dyson, in 1989. I was a great fan of James's, and loved his attitude to life.

The orange helmet which caused a few political problems while racing Formula 3000 in 1990.

A controversial debut. On my way into the points and the headlines with the Jordan-Hart during the 1993 Japanese Grand Prix at Suzuka.

Above: At home with the GTO which, in my opinion, is one of the best road cars ever made by Ferrari.

Below: My first outing for Ferrari. Testing the 1995 car at Estoril in December.

Posing for the pre-season group photograph in Melbourne. It would be interesting to lay a bet on how many drivers would be wearing the same team colours the following season.

Would you believe it? Finishing third in Melbourne at the end of my first race for Ferrari – what a fabulous start!

Over my head. As I celebrate on the podium in Melbourne, the colour of the flag being raised high above me is about to cause a furore in certain quarters.

Looking forward to a challenging season with my new team.

Fending off a McLaren (main picture) during a very difficult weekend at Interlagos in Brazil. Things got off to an embarrassing start when I crashed the car (inset) on my first lap out of the pits.

Serious consultation with Ferrari engineers, Gustav Brunner (centre) and Luca Baldisserri.

Eddie Jordan, the man who gave me my Formula 1 break – and likes to remind me about it!

As usual, I'm coping manfully with the pressures of the job, this time in Argentina.

Grovewood Securities owned Brands Hatch and Webb was therefore involved with the awards. The suggestion was that if I wanted to win the major Cellnet Award, it might be a good idea if I forgot about the appeal. So I dropped the protest. And I didn't win the award.

Everyone said Webb had actually done me a favour. The Grovewood Awards had been running for more than twenty years and they were the kiss of death to a driver's career. In 1987, the top prize went to Derek Higgins. He has hardly been heard of since and I certainly don't know where he was in April 1996. As for me, I was in Germany, driving a Ferrari in the European Grand Prix.

CHAPTER 6

The Gap Grows in Germany

I was told that the summer weather in Ireland was going to be fantastic. The prediction was based on a sound meteorological principle, something along the lines of dolphins having arrived early in Bantry Bay. So that was it – Ireland was in for a gorgeous summer.

As far as I was concerned, the dolphins had not arrived early enough. In between Argentina and the first race in Europe, my search for sunshine had proved fruitless. I had been testing at Monza in Italy immediately after my return from Buenos Aires and then I went to Dublin, where it rained non-stop for three days. I actually had a very enjoyable weekend socially but the weather was really depressing. Each time I stepped outside, it was pouring. You can only take so much of that. I went back to Bologna and decided to stay there until someone rang me from Ireland to say it was quite true about the effect of the Bantry Bay dolphins.

I never did get the call before going to the Nurburgring in Germany for the European Grand Prix. Everyone came prepared for bad weather mainly because, on our last visit to this corner of the Eifel mountains the previous October, it had been bloody cold. That was the weekend when everyone in the paddock was coming to terms with the surprise news that I had signed for Ferrari. Six months later and the novelty value had definitely worn off. The sun was shining and people were looking for results. The truth was, we were still struggling to make the car work.

The post-Argentina test at Monza had proved very little. Straightaway, we had a gearbox problem which seriously restricted our running. We tested a new floor and that was a step in the right direction; it stabilised the rear of the car going into corners. But that was about as far as it went because of the lack of running. Apart from the gearbox problems, the test was affected by the fact that Monza had hardly been used since the winter and the track was very dirty. Michael then tested for two days and he tried a revised front wing which I would subsequently use at the Nurburgring.

As far as I was concerned, the wing solved one problem and produced another. It made the rear of the car less nervous turning in to the corner but gave me very bad understeer on the way out. In simple terms, the car wanted to go straight on rather than follow the line of the exit. To get over that, I had to slow down too much and attempt to make a straight line out of the exit in order not to load up the front of the car and produce understeer. It was not the quickest way through the corner by any means.

The problem was, because of a lack of testing, we were not familiar with this new problem and we didn't react quickly enough during practice at the Nurburgring. We should have started to make major changes in order to get rid of the understeer, but we didn't know whether it was my driving, the circuit or the car. Unfortunately, there was not enough time to find out. Having said that, I managed to do a really good lap during qualifying and took seventh place on the grid; another few tenths of a second and I would have been fourth quickest, which, all things considered, would have been a brilliant job.

Seventh felt good – except that Michael was a lot quicker and I couldn't really understand why. He had done a lot of testing and it could have been that he had his car set up much better. Also, this was his home race and that is a factor which should never be overlooked. Even so, I was a lot further off his pace than I expected to be.

Apart from Argentina, I had been within half a second of Michael everywhere we raced. I could understand the difference between us in Buenos Aires because Michael had been wringing the car's neck. But I was disappointed with the Nurburgring; I put it down to the amount of testing Michael had been doing. He had been getting better, while I was getting worse.

I had no complaint with the reason behind that. The situation had been forced on us because of the problems with the gearbox; we didn't have enough gearboxes and, as soon as a revised one became available, Michael had first call. It didn't make sense to give the gearbox to me.

In any case, I had been concentrating on dealing with a problem which was not affecting Michael. Each time I hit a bump, I was getting about 20mm of throttle movement, which obviously I didn't want. My foot would shoot forward and start an oscillation. It was also happening quite a lot when I changed gear. We tried various seats and, at the Nurburgring, we were working on the ninth different heel rest in an attempt to adjust the angle of my foot on the throttle pedal. It had been a nightmare in Argentina, particularly as there were so many bumps on that particular track but, by the time we reached Germany, we were beginning to get on top of the problem, more through luck than anything else. The position we finally found for my foot was not the most logical. It was not comfortable either but it worked. Besides, there was no alternative.

Going into the race I was concerned because both Michael and I had been having clutch problems throughout weekend; we had been stalling the engine while trying to leave the pits. I was really worried about the start – and with due cause, as it would turn out. I let out the clutch, the car took off and then the revs died. I tried to slip the clutch but it disengaged completely, the revs shot to maximum and then the engine just went 'bluuugggh' when I pulled the next gear. It was the worst start possible.

When I finally got going, I was in ninth place, stuck behind a Jordan. If Damon Hill, who was a couple of places ahead of me in his Williams, could not get past the other Jordan, then there was not much chance for the Ferrari, one of the slowest cars on the straight. Certainly, there was no chance whatsoever when the engine began to misfire and I started to fall further back. Olivier Panis tried to overtake me but he made a mess of it and hit my car which, in a way, was quite good because my race was over anyway and the incident put the Ligier driver out of the race and stopped him from scoring a couple of points.

Jacques Villeneuve in the Williams scored his first Grand Prix victory. I thought it was a shame that he didn't win the opening race of the season because he had done a bloody good job in Melbourne. Apart from that, I found it very difficult to say anything constructive about Jacques's performances in general. The Williams drivers had such an easy job in the opening races thanks to the rest of the teams needing to get our acts together. To my mind, a number of drivers could have won in a Williams. That's what it had come down to. It was the same with my third place in Melbourne; anyone could have done the job under the circumstances.

I found it amusing that people had been surprised when Villeneuve proved to be competitive in Australia and then won in Germany. Just how useless did they think he was? He had been on pole position in Melbourne and on the front row at the Nurburgring. He was in a Williams, so he was either going to finish first or second. Why the surprise? The lack of understanding within F1 can be quite mind-boggling.

I had raced against Jacques in Japan but I felt he had changed quite a lot since then, becoming much more serious. In Japan, he had been heavily into having a lot of fun but, in Formula 1, he was focused on what he was doing. Having said that, it was very difficult to tell whether or not he had improved as a driver. All I could say was that he had been very clever with his moves through Indycar racing and then into Formula 1. I felt he was as good as anyone, apart from Michael Schumacher.

At the Nurburgring, Michael had stood out once again and the move to Ferrari was allowing him to prove a point or two. When he was with Benetton, there were complaints that Benetton ran a one-car team for Michael's benefit. In the first few races of 1996, Jean Alesi had been consistently quicker than Gerhard Berger – but there were no comments about a one-car team for Alesi.

I could have said that Ferrari were are running a one-car team if only because Michael had been doing all the testing. But I was being given as good a car as Michael and it was up to me to do the business. As I said, that proved more difficult than usual in Germany, mainly because Michael had been absolutely flying. He looked really good and people began to think that we had made a big step forward with the car. In actual fact, the Williams-Renaults were slow and that flattered the Ferrari as Michael finished a close second to Villeneuve. Of course, this also prompted people to question our working relationship. The general feeling seemed to be that the discrepancy in our performances was bound to cause some sort of rift between Michael and I.

Our rapport had been getting better and better with each race. We were not socialising very much because Michael was either testing somewhere or he had gone back to his apartment in Monaco. If I had lived in Monte Carlo as well, we would have been in each other's company more often but, even then, social contact would have been limited because we did not have much in common and lived totally different lives.

It was mainly business at the races of course and we were completely open with each other. For instance, Michael had no objection to me looking at the traces produced by the telemetry from his car. The traces show absolutely everything: steering input, brake pressure, throttle opening, revs, G forces, everything. You can read it like a book; it's not too baffling. I could see that Michael had been doing certain things with his driving style, so I tried them for myself in Australia. It had not been a problem but, in the races which followed, it turned out to be a struggle because of the way the car reacted. I put that down to being comparatively unfamiliar with the F310. As I explained earlier, I had spent two or three days with the car at Fiorano before the start of the season. I had not been doing anything particularly important but at least I was in the car for a period and got the feel of it. After the first four races, I hadn't had the chance to get to the bottom of just why I was no longer able to stay close to Michael's lap times.

Michael works very hard; his output is phenomenal. I don't think he necessarily has to do it because, no matter where we are, he can go quickly straight away. He does not need to spend a lot of effort chipping away at his lap time; he is second fastest, or thereabouts, almost immediately and he stays there. At the end of the day, the guy is just plain quick. He puts in a lot of work and he may go through a huge number of tiny details but, invariably, he goes out and does the time within one lap.

Despite the misgivings of observers outside the team, I was not upset by the discrepancy between us. I was not happy about it, but I knew that a solid two or three days spent testing would help. Unfortunately, because of the shortage of parts, I knew that would not happen for five or six weeks. I would be doing one day here and there but that would not be enough. You need two or three days in order to begin to fully understand the car and make forward progress. Then you go to each race with that set up and start work from a known base-line. At the Nurburgring, I had been guessing all the time; I had nothing substantial to work on.

Having said that, I had to recognise that perhaps Michael had lifted his performance, although I found that difficult to believe. If he was always quick from the word go then very little would have changed since we started testing together after the pair of us had joined Ferrari. I could comfort myself with the thought that I had been only about three tenths of a second off Michael's time during the winter. At Fiorano I had been slightly quicker. I qualified ahead of him at the first race; we had been separated by just three-hundredths of a second in the warm-up although, in the race, he had an advantage because my front wing had been damaged and my car was understeering badly. There is no doubt that Michael had an edge, but it had never been as pronounced as it was in Germany.

I had time to reflect on that a few days later while taking part in the filming of a commercial for Shell at the Mugello circuit in Italy. It was pretty simple work from my point of view. I spent most of my time driving into the pits; to be honest, it was boring as hell. I just don't believe people who say they love acting. For commercials, the film crews need to take the same shot so many times just to get it right. I can understand how an actor would enjoy performing on stage in the West End or on Broadway; I can see the excitement in that. You get one go at it; you've literally got to perform. But as for acting in front of the cameras, it's mind-numbing. You've got to want the fame and, I suppose, the money. Perhaps making a film is different from shooting a commercial, but it's not for me. I was doing my acting bit as well as driving the car. I found it easy. I could be a star, no problem at all! But, based on that experience, I would rather be a Grand Prix driver, thanks very much.

One of the down-sides of doing my job is the need to be fit. It is something I have always hated, even as a kid. I used to swim a lot, an hour before and after school each day, but I didn't work hard enough because I didn't particularly enjoy it. I was actually quite good. I was County Champion, second in Ulster, sixth in Ireland, winner of lots of competitions. But, despite all that, I didn't find it much fun.

I got a bigger kick from riding my bicycle. I would race a friend called William around the paths of a local estate. There was little to choose between us; we would race all evening on these little footpaths, sliding the bikes round corners, just flat out all night. I was very fit because of that. When you are a kid, you've got all this energy you don't know what to do with and I used to burn mine in the swimming pool and charging around on my bike rather than on the school playing fields. I ran cross country and played rugby but didn't particularly enjoy either of them. I didn't really like any form of exercise, to be honest.

Even when I started racing, I did nothing about my physical preparation. Looking back on it now, I realise I was very unfit. When I finally started, I remember going for a three-mile run and having to stop about five times. The next day, I stopped twice; the day after that, I stopped once; the next day, I didn't stop at all. The fitness programme only began when I went into Formula 3. I was told I should be better prepared. They said I was on my way to becoming a professional racing driver and I ought to act accordingly. Then I met James Hunt…

CHAPTER 7

A Drop of the Hard Stuff

I first met James Hunt through his role as consultant to Marlboro. I had seen James race, of course. In fact, I had managed to get myself onto the top of the control tower at Brands Hatch on that famous day in 1976 when he was involved in a controversial incident at the start of the British Grand Prix. The organisers wanted to throw him out but the crowd went mad and, wisely perhaps, the officials decided James could take the restart after all. He won the race, was later disqualified, but went on to become World Champion that year by one point.

I was a great fan. I liked his attitude; James was very much his own man. When I was invited to test for the 1988 Marlboro Formula 3 drive, I really wanted to do Formula Ford 2000 first. But I was offered the drive and James and everyone else said I should accept and move straight to Formula 3 which, for me, was a massive step.

I took the advice and joined the team run by Dick Bennetts. Winning the Marlboro drive brought some street credibility and a nice pair of red overalls! Everything was more or less paid for although I was supposed to find a certain amount of money, but I never did. I had the best car, the best preparation – but not the best engine. The Alfa Romeo was not as powerful as the Toyota which JJ Lehto would use to win the British title. I finished second six times but, apart from the struggle in the races, it was great fun. Dick Bennetts had a good bunch of guys working for his team and I learned a lot about setting up the car and how to go racing. In fact, I realised just how much I didn't know.

At the end of the season I went to Macau for the most important F3 race of the year. The Macau Grand Prix was a high-profile event and, for me, it was also a good excuse to travel abroad. I had been to France once on holiday, and to Canada when I was eight years old. But that was about it. This was my first proper trip abroad and it was an impressive way to start. Coming in to land at Hong Kong's Kai Tak airport, where the plane would appear to swoop down between the buildings, was an amazing spectacle, particularly if your previous experiences had been limited to Belfast airport and Heathrow. Then the hour on the jetfoil across to Macau which, at the time, was a magical place. It's gone downhill over the years but, in 1988, I thought it was incredible. The 3.8 mile Guia track is similar in some ways to Monaco, but much faster. There is a long seafront section and a winding inland run along a hillside; all told, it is a fantastic challenge. The organisers, led by Teddy Yipp, a very wealthy businessman and motor sport fan , could not do enough for you. All expenses were paid.

I was driving my regular car, prepared by Dick Bennetts but entered under the Theodore Racing banner by Sidney Taylor, an Irishman who had been involved in the sport for more than twenty years. Sid has the dubious honour of being the first person ever to pay me for driving a racing car. I received £1,000 while the top guys, such as Bertrand Gachot and Martin Donnelly, got about £8,000 and Lehto was on around £5,000. Despite the pay discrepancy, I put my car on pole.

The sudden jump in competitiveness for the Ralt-Alfa Romeo had come from the fact that we could use aviation fuel in Macau. In Britain, everyone had been restricted to 99 octane fuel but we found that the Alfa Romeo definitely liked the increase to a 106 octane rating! It was the first time all season that I felt I was on a par with everyone else.

Nobody had taken much notice of me on the first day of practice, mainly because I had been about seventeenth fastest and three seconds off the pace. I remember thinking: 'Jeez, *three* seconds! Where do I find that?' We softened the set-up of the car – it had been a bit too stiff for the bumps – and, the next day, I put on a new set of tyres. It worked wonders: pole position on my first visit with a lap of 2 minutes 22.99 seconds. Then I crashed.

I had just left the pits for another run when Sid Taylor hung out the pit board showing 2:32.1. It was, in fact, the time I had recorded on my first lap out of the pits – a piece of information which is of no use to anyone! Not realising that, I misread the signal. I thought: 'Two-twenty-two point one … someone's beaten my time! I've got to go for it!' I tore into the first corner and clipped the barrier on the exit. That was it. Bang! The front left-hand corner took the impact. I was pretty unhappy because it was the first time I had damaged a car during the season.

The race was run in two heats and I won the first part easily. I didn't make a good start at the beginning of heat two. Jean Alesi – whose place at Ferrari I would take seven years later – and I were side-by-side going into the first corner with the Swedish driver, Rickard Rydell, trying to make the most of my poor start by coming up the inside. Rydell and I touched and that spun me into the barrier. My race was over. But at least I had taken pole position and my fastest lap of the race was not beaten in the second heat. Although I was disappointed with the final outcome, I had created the right impression at the end of an otherwise mediocre season.

A few weeks before going to Macau, I had been invited to take part in a Formula 3000 test organised by Marlboro at Imola. I was up against Emanuele Naspetti and Erik Comas, the Italian and French Formula 3 champions. I had never been to the Italian circuit before, whereas Naspetti lived just down the road in Ancona. There was quite a bit at stake here because we were going for one seat in the Pacific team, which was making the move into Formula 3000 after winning the Formula 3 championship with Lehto. Naturally, JJ was moving up the ladder with his old team.

We were each given a 25-lap stint and I went last. I didn't have a problem with the transition to a more powerful engine and, to my surprise, I was the quickest of three. The people from Marlboro said: 'Go to Macao; the race is a bit of a lottery but do a good job during qualifying and you'll be looking pretty good.' So, as recounted, I went to Macau and put it on pole. By the end of November 1988, it was more or less agreed that I had the Formula 3000 drive with the Pacific team.

Apart from the test, my experience of Formula 3000 had been limited to a visit as a spectator to the final race of the season at Dijon in France. And I didn't learn much that weekend thanks to the antics of my guide and mentor, James Hunt.

I met him at Heathrow. The first thing he did was visit the Duty Free shop and buy a bottle of blue vodka. When we landed in Paris, he nipped off to meet two girls at a railway station. As it turned out, the TGV express trains were cancelled due to a strike and we had to catch a slow train loaded with naval conscripts on their way to Marseilles. It took us about five hours to get to Dijon – by which time there was nothing left of the vodka.

We crawled through the doors of the hotel. Luckily, it was very late by then and the motor racing people had gone to bed. So we retired to James's room, where he began playing Beethoven at full blast on his portable stereo. James ignored the banging on the walls and the ceiling until someone arrived from reception and told us to stop the party because it was 3 am. And James was supposed to be instructing me on how to be a professional racing driver…

I went down for breakfast the following morning and met Volker Weidler, who was racing for the Marlboro-supported F3000 team that weekend. Volker said: 'Last night was unbelievable. I never got any sleep at all. The people in the room beside me were partying all night. I had to ring reception to get it stopped.'

'Jeez, Volker,' I said. 'That's awful.' He didn't find out who the culprits were until about four years later. We were racing in Japan and, one night, I told him. His reaction was incredible. He said: 'I knew it! I knew Marlboro wanted me out. They sent you to party and keep me awake all night before the race.' He really believed that.

Volker had been driving for Onyx. The Marlboro-backed team then moved into Formula 1 in 1989, which was one of the reasons why the Philip Morris money had gone to Pacific and led Weidler to believe James's excesses in Dijon had been part of an elaborate plot. It was the result of a five-hour train journey and a bottle of vodka; nothing more and nothing less.

Pacific Racing had done well in everything they had tackled before. The team from Norfolk would have Reynard chassis, Mugen engines from Japan, backing from Marlboro and Lehto and I as drivers. According to most pre-season forecasts, Pacific Racing was looking good.

I out-qualified JJ at the first race and that seemed to surprise everyone, particularly within the team. It made life difficult because Pacific was built around Lehto and even though I was quicker than him more often than not (I think the ratio was 6–3 that season), he remained the favourite – which hacked me off just a little.

To make matters worse, I was black-flagged during the third round of the championship on the streets of Pau in France. According to the officials, I was blocking another driver – who just happened to be a Frenchman. To hear them talk, you would have thought I had been weaving all over the place. In actual fact, I had been driving on exactly the same line every lap. My car was so bad over the bumps that I couldn't even contemplate taking the outside line when braking for the corners. The guy behind me may have been quicker but it was up to him to find a way around the outside.

I was hauled before the Stewards and fined $5,000, which was unbelievable. The inconsistency shown by representatives of the FIA, the sports governing body, typified the system at the time. A week before, during the Monaco Grand Prix, Rene Arnoux had been slapped on the wrist for blocking the leaders as they tried to lap him. I was fighting for a place, not being lapped, and yet Arnoux had effectively ruined the Monaco Grand Prix by costing Alain Prost, the second-place man, ten seconds in five laps during his chase of Ayrton Senna. And Arnoux merely received a reprimand. I was fined a serious amount of money, which I didn't have.

I was actually living off money made from buying and selling road cars. Marlboro wanted me to stop my wheeling and dealing; they weren't very impressed when I nearly missed a race because I was dropping off a car to a potential customer on the way to the circuit! Marlboro's argument was that I was meant to find sponsorship. They had given me a free drive and space to sell on the car and on my overalls. Most drivers had managed to come up with some money, but I could not find any. I did try – not massively hard, I must admit – but the problem was, I had no contacts. I had been plucked from Formula Ford and, all of a sudden, I was on the Marlboro ladder. Marlboro tried to help, as did David Marren, a Dublin-based associate of Philip Morris but, at the end of the day, who was going to sponsor someone from Northern Ireland?

A lot of people believed I had a free budget; some thought I was earning £40–50,000 a year! Hector Lester, the estate agent from Portadown who had lent me his car for the Formula Ford festival back in 1985, helped me out, as did Ian Adamson, a friend of my Dad. Ian, a doctor from Conlig, our local village, wrote a successful book and kindly gave me some of the proceeds. That was the sum total of the support. There had been one or two businessmen who promised help, but the money was never delivered. It was always 'Next year, next year'.

This year, 1989, had been a disaster. I had finished on the podium once but at least I had scored more points than Lehto even if it did mean I was a poor ninth in the championship and JJ was back in thirteenth place. Lehto, who was a Ferrari test driver for a while, went Formula 1 racing with Onyx. I was left hanging in mid air. Then Eddie Jordan called.

Alesi had won the 1989 championship in a Jordan Reynard and we quickly did a deal which meant I would now be in the yellow Camel colours rather than the red and white of Marlboro. As usual, Eddie had grandiose ideas. There were to be three drivers in all: myself, Heinz-Harald Frentzen and Emanuele Naspetti. Frentzen was quite young and, in any case, he was going out with Corrina Betsch, who would later become Michael Schumacher's wife. But Naspetti was very good fun; I had a great time with him. At least it made up for a dismal first half of the 1990 season.

I scored just one point in the first four races. We went testing before the fifth round at Monza and tried the car with a front roll bar. It made a big difference and, the stiffer the bar the faster I went. I finished second at Monza, fourth in the next race and then won at Hockenheim. I scored more points than anyone else from Monza on, but the damage had been done by poor results early in the season. I finished third in the championship which, all things considered, was not too bad because the Reynard was no match for the Lola which Erik Comas used to almost cruise to the title that year. When a driver finds himself in a car which is not on the pace, there is little he can do. The only answer, in my case, was to beat my team-mates and to have fun along the way. I managed to do both.

I was living in Oxford in what could best be described as a rat hole. Emanuele, whose parents were quite wealthy, was staying in a penthouse apartment, which he let me use whenever he wasn't in the country. It was very decent of him to do that, particularly when he knew what I would be getting up to.

We had been to Japan together to do a sportscar race. This was a deal arranged by Eddie Jordan which, naturally, was a nice little earner for EJ. Naspetti and I stayed in a hotel which was just unbelievable. Emanuele had the porn channel running on the television and he decided he wanted a massage. I had never experienced anything like this before. I asked him what he would do if the masseuse was an old dog; he assured me she would be very nice. I said I would let the lady in and then disappear for a while.

There was a knock on the door. I opened it and an 80-year-old woman walked in! I tried to get away as quickly as possible but, once Emanuele had taken everything on board, he dragged me back in. This poor woman was wondering what on earth was happening; there was porn on the television and the two of us were having a scrap, trying to get out through the door.

Naspetti would not let me go. He rang for another woman to come to the room and sort me out. So we had this ridiculous situation where the two of us were having a massage while, in the background, we could hear the sound of action coming from the blue movie while these two old women were working away. They were obviously taking the whole thing very seriously and we were laughing our heads off.

The guy from the advertising agency working with the team took us to a club in Tokyo, where he said we could have a proper massage, but not with old ladies. I was quite naive and said I didn't want to know. Naspetti said he would go first. His lady arrived – and she was not old, but she was not beautiful either. As he disappeared upstairs, I thought: 'Well at least he has the ugly one'. My escort arrived. She was no better. Of course, it would have been considered to be very rude, an insult to the sponsor who was footing the bill, if we had refused. I had my massage and then, as they say in the *News of the World*, made my excuses and left pretty quickly. I met Emanuele on the way out! The Japanese must have thought we were a couple of premature European ejaculators!

We were supposed to race a Porsche 956. Neither of us were very happy about that because that sportscar did not have a good reputation from the safety point of view. I remember asking one of the mechanics if there was anything more to go on the front of the car. It looked like the driver had to put his feet in a biscuit tin; there was no protection worth talking about. He said, no, that was it. I didn't fancy having a frontal impact in that car but, fortunately, fog came down before the race was due to start and the whole thing was cancelled. It was one of the happiest days of my life.

It was a relief to return to Europe and continue the struggle with the Reynard F3000 car. The Lola won seven races that year compared to four for the Reynard, a situation which could be compared with the domination of the Williams-Renault in Grand Prix racing in 1996. Having watched the Williams drivers win all four races so far, there seemed no reason to believe that they would not walk off with Round 5 on Ferrari's home ground at Imola. What we needed was someone to arrive at the Williams drivers' hotel with vodka and Beethoven at three in the morning...

CHAPTER 8

A Bit of a Pain

There is no end to what a driver will do for that extra tenth of a second. Michael and I had been aware for some time that our helmets had been getting in the way of the opening to the engine airbox directly above our heads. When you look at photographs, our heads were not exactly blocking the airbox, but it is amazing the difference even the slightest intrusion on the airflow can make to the way the engine breathes. It can cost a couple of kilometres per hour in performance. When you are measuring lap times in hundredths of a second over a distance of around three miles, then those extra few kph are worth chasing.

Both Michael and I tried putting our heads to one side rather than sitting upright while going down the straight. It does help even though, at first, it is disorientating as you travel at 170 mph with your head cocked to the right or the left. You soon get used to it although, from the outside, it looks as though the driver has fallen asleep with his head propped up against the side of the cockpit. If we had to drive like that continually, then we would be walking around the paddock with a permanent crick in our necks, not to mention being arrested for adopting a suggestive pose. I had tried to ease the situation by changing my driving position in order to sit a fraction lower in the car.

I have always had back trouble while driving, partly because I have a spine which is quite long for someone of my height. Back trouble is widespread among racing drivers. Derek Daly, a Dubliner who used to race Formula 1 and Indycars, told me to put an arch in my back and give it support. That helped to cure his problem. I could never understand why that should ease the discomfort, but I took his advice while racing in Formula 3000 and it worked. Since then, my seat backs had been made in an 'S' shape but now I was prepared to take the arch out of my back, if only to allow a lower seating position. When I tried the new seat while the car was stationary, it felt comfortable. It was a bit sore during practice, but not enough to worry me. In any case, I was too busy trying to improve the car.

The problem with understeer on the F310 had been so acute at the Nurburgring that we decided we were going to get rid of it at all costs. We made the rear of the car much stiffer, to such an extent that the rear springs on my car were three times harder than those used by Michael. It made the car feel very twitchy at the back – but there was no understeer!

Overall, the car was good enough to give me sixth fastest time during qualifying. I had actually been in fourth place until the final run and I was confident of being able to maintain that because I usually leave my big effort until the end. When I went out for the last time, the car felt really strange. I was actually slower than before and, worse than that, David Coulthard and Jean Alesi went quicker. When the mechanics checked the car, they discovered that a rear damper had gone so, in that respect, I was quite pleased with sixth place. Put in another way, I would have felt even happier with my performance had Michael not given Ferrari pole position in the final minutes of qualifying.

It was a fantastic performance by Michael. The crowd went berserk since this was the first pole for Ferrari at Imola since 1983. As far as I was concerned, the 1.3-second discrepancy between the two Ferraris was yet another sign of the increasing gap between Michael and I. Michael's lap was quite a talking point in the paddock but, in the debrief afterwards, we knew that our grid positions would be, to a certain extent, irrelevant because we were continuing to have problems with the clutch. Bearing in mind my terrible getaway two weeks before in Germany, I was not counting on a good start, and Michael did not have high hopes of making the most of his pole position.

Basically, the clutch on the F310 was not working properly. It was unpredictable in so far as the bite point would move and, when it came in, the effect would be very sudden, very sharp. I found this to be very frustrating because I pride myself with having made good starts throughout my career. And yet, in the season so far, I had made just one half-decent start, and that was in Melbourne. Since then, the clutch had been really bad. Imola was to be no exception.

I dropped to about ninth place within seconds of the start . Once the race settled down – there had been a bit of confusion at the second corner and it was no surprise to find that Alesi had been in the thick of it – I moved up a place and then concentrated on finding a decent rhythm. I was able to do that and, for the first time this season, I felt I was really driving well. Then I caught up with Alesi. He seemed to be struggling and the only way I could get by was once he had disappeared into the pits and I had a clear run for several laps before my stop was due. Rejoining in sixth place, I was catching Barrichello hand over fist; I was pleased with that. In fact, looking at the lap times, only Damon Hill and Michael were getting round Imola faster than me.

The second and final round of pit stops allowed me to get ahead of the Jordan and move into what had now become fourth place. I was looking seriously at making that third because I was closing in on Gerhard Berger's Benetton. Then I caught up with Pedro Diniz, who was a lap down in the Ligier. Unfortunately, he held me up for four or five laps and that cost me several seconds. In the end, I had to be content with fourth place, Hill having won the race with Michael second and Berger third. As I took the flag, I made the mistake of thinking my weekend's work was over. In fact, another battle was about to start.

Unbeknown to me, Michael had serious brake trouble. I noticed that he had pulled over to the side of the road after crossing the line. Since the crowd had begun to climb over the fences, I just assumed all the other cars were going to park there. I had no idea of what lay in store.

As I began to climb out, a mob had already surrounded the car. As soon as I was on my feet, they were pulling and pushing really hard.

They were trying to take my helmet off without undoing the strap. People were making a big thing out of shaking my hand, but I could feel them trying to remove the glove. At one point I thought they wanted to lift me up, but then I realised they were actually trying to get on to my shoulders. They were jumping on top of me, crowding in from all sides. It was total madness.

By now, I had suddenly remembered about my new seat and my back problem. After about five laps of the race I had been in absolute agony. I was having to pull up my left leg and try and move it to the side, just to find some relief. After about twenty-five laps, the pain was so intense that my back became numb. There was no problem after that; I couldn't feel a thing. By the end of the race, the two main muscles running down either side of my back were standing out like silicone implants. A few minutes after climbing from the car, they had tightened up and were hurting like hell. And now I was having to deal with this human scrum. I couldn't really understand it. If they were being enthusiastic, then why where they thumping me? It was almost menacing.

We had been warned at the drivers' pre-race briefing that a track invasion was likely. There is little a driver can do except pull to one side, get out of the car and hope for the best. At least, with Michael nearby, I knew there would be someone to rescue us.

Sure enough, a car appeared, picked up Michael – and left me standing in the middle of this mob. Then another car arrived, the officials looked at me, and drove on. Obviously, they didn't recognise me! They were all rushing to pick up Michael, who was quite clearly The Man after his performance that weekend. Nonetheless, I wasn't very impressed. I thought: 'What a bunch of useless chaps'. Except I didn't put it quite like that! I tried to run towards the pits but it was impossible. A couple of security guards were attempting to help but they could do very little in the face of the increasing chaos.

This was the downside of the fanatical Ferrari support. There had been incredible scenes before the start of the race when the drivers went round in open-top cars on a parade lap. The crowd went crazy. It made me feel I was really doing something worthwhile and yet it was slightly embarrassing. I felt I was struggling to hang in there. They were cheering me on and yet I was not capable of doing the job I should have been able to do.

There is no denying that matters were not helped – from my point of view – by Michael's success. He was doing things his way and I had the feeling that I was half-expected to do things that way as well. But that's not me. As I said before, I was not convinced that his way of operation actually made that much difference when it came to the bottom line. He would be quick the minute he took to the track and then he would not go that much faster. So why the lengthy discussions with the engineers and designers? That didn't seem right to me. It didn't add up. But, of course, I could not make any sort of judgement until I had been for a decent test. And that was still some way off because of the shortage of gearboxes. The Monaco Grand Prix would come first.

It made a very pleasant change to drive to a race instead of going through the usual hassle associated with airports and flying. I suppose it shows how much things have changed; thirty years ago it was not unusual for racing drivers to motor to the European races in their Jaguars and Ford Zephyrs; flying was something of a luxury. Now, of course, flying is like getting on a bus; in fact, it is not as easy as that. So, I really enjoyed getting behind the wheel of my Alfa for the journey west from Bologna to Monte Carlo. The scenery was stunning in places and, of course, I could have my CDs on full blast. The Cranberries, Oasis and Van Morrison are among my favourites.

In fact, I had met Van Morrison's girlfriend, Michelle Rocha, in Lillie's Bordello night club and she told me they were planning to move near to where I lived. You can imagine how I felt when Van Morrison bought a big property on the land just below my house. I didn't actually come face to face with him but I had a bit of a shock one day when driving my car. I was with Nicola, my girlfriend, and we were listening to the news headlines on the local radio station. The news reader said: 'Van Morrison's girlfriend in secret tryst with local race ace.'

Nicola and I looked at each other without saying a word. My conscience was absolutely clear, but you never know what the media are going to say next. When they got to the detail of the story, it turned out that Michelle Rocha had allegedly been having an affair with someone from the world of *horse* racing. Nicola and I burst out laughing. I don't suppose Van Morrison and his lady saw the funny side of that story. In fact, they moved out not long after.

I always have time for Irish folk music. I really love that. To my mind, there is nothing better than sitting in a bar as a handful of musicians get going with fiddles, guitars and penny whistles. Even as far afield as Tokyo, I found a place where they specialised in what I call the 'diddly-dee' music. It was brilliant. So I had a bit of that while on the road because there would be little time for relaxing once I reached Monte Carlo.

People have mixed views on Monaco as a Grand Prix venue. Some say it is out of date and dangerous and should have no place in modern Formula 1; the streets are too narrow and the walls and barriers too close; you can't overtake. I think it's a great circuit. It's very difficult for all the reasons mentioned and it places great demands on the driver. It's all go in every sense. More than that, it's good fun to drive around. Places like the chicanes at the swimming pool are excellent. The entry is blind with high walls and barriers on either side. It's quick through there and requires total commitment by the driver.

After the first day of practice on Thursday, I was really pleased to see that I was as quick as Michael around the swimming pool section. Unfortunately I was losing out elsewhere; he was much faster on the entry and exit of the very quick run through Casino Square at the top of the hill. By the time qualifying had finished on Saturday, Michael was on pole position once again and I was seventh quickest, 1.2 seconds behind. Once again, the gap between us was greater than I would have liked but the reasons for it were the same as before.

My car had felt pretty good straight away on Thursday. We had made a change to the set-up and that brought an improvement. But when we tried further alterations, we only succeeded in getting lost; no matter what we tried on the car, I ended up doing roughly the same lap time. We did, however, find time by making the rear of the car much more stable. We knew how to fix one or two particular problems, but we didn't know how to fix them all. It simply verified everything I had been saying about the need to go testing in order to get the whole picture.

During the weekend, I had been asked to attend an official press conference to answer questions from the floor. One journalist, who specialises in asking the difficult and sometimes controversial questions, wanted to know whether or not I was becoming frustrated by my lack of testing and the fact that, once again, I was slower than Michael.

In my view, there's no point in asking a question unless it's awkward; I don't have a problem with that. The only problem was, everyone had been asking this particular question. There was not much I could say. There had been very little testing for me because there was a shortage of gearboxes, and that was outside my control. I signed the contract with Ferrari knowing what I was letting myself in for. It was true that I didn't think it was going to be as bad as it had been, but it was a fact; it was happening and I couldn't change anything. The team as a whole was on target, scoring points and, so long as that remained the case, then we would be happy with what we were doing.

In fact, it seemed to me that the journalists were more concerned about the situation than I was. I think they were hoping that I would criticise Michael; slag him off as we say in Ireland! I had no reason to do that because, at the end of the day, he was looking after his own interests just as I was looking after mine.

I was asked whether, in retrospect, I was happy with my decision to leave Jordan for Ferrari. I agreed that Jordan was going better than before but, at the time of the Monaco Grand Prix, I had scored more points than the two Jordan drivers put together. True, it was not going as well as it could have done at Ferrari, but I had to look at the situation I had been in before and the one I was in now. I was obviously on a much better deal at Ferrari and I had been scoring more points than I could have managed with Jordan.

I had really enjoyed Jordan as a team, and we had a fantastic time together. In my opinion, Ian Phillips, the commercial manager, was a star; Eddie Jordan was funny; the whole team was a gas and they do a bloody good job, too. But there's no doubt in my mind that, at the end of the day, they needed more technical people in the team.

People had been saying to me that Michael is successful because he works so hard, the inference being that, if I did likewise, then I would be like him. I don't believe that's the case. I sometimes wonder if he needs to go through everything in such incredible detail in order to be successful. I may be wrong but I think Michael is just quick. And that's all there is to it.

I managed to take a break from the technicalities of Formula 1 by taking part in what I could best describe as a fashion show staged by Cerruti, who support Ferrari. This involved young actors and actresses parading about in Cerruti clothes. Chantal Cerruti invited me along; she's a really, really nice woman. I had previously done a fashion shoot for her and *Class* magazine. It meant being on the beach in Cannes, wearing different clothes and posing for the camera. They had an excellent photographer, and I really enjoyed the show.

I suppose that represents the jet-set image people have of Grand Prix drivers, particularly at Monaco. The belief is that this race is one big social whirl. That may be true for most people, but not for the drivers. I did manage to have dinner with Ian Phillips on the Tuesday evening. It's always good to see Ian again; he's an amusing character and a mine of information. Whether his stories are true or not is another thing, but he churns them out with great enthusiasm and everyone takes them on board.

On Thursday evening, Nicola arrived in Monaco with a couple of friends. I said I would meet them in Stars and Bars, a popular haunt on the quayside, just behind the paddock. But, when it came to the time, I was just too tired to contemplate it. Apparently everyone had great fun. I was in bed. Asleep. So much for the romance.

I might have thought about joining the scene at Stars and Bars had I still been driving for Jordan. EJ didn't care what I did, so long as I performed. I didn't feel it was right to be seen there in my new role at Ferrari. I had to accept that I am much more in the public eye with such a top team. I had to take all these things into consideration.

That's the way life is for a Ferrari driver. I certainly felt restricted in my movements. There is always someone watching, waiting for you to make a mistake. I felt like a monk. It's not much fun. In fact, it was a pain, but completely different to the discomfort I had experienced at Imola. I simply had to play it carefully until the results started to come in. Only then would I be able to relax. But that seemed to be a long way off when I went to the grid for the Monaco Grand Prix.

CHAPTER 9

Monaco: Home in a Boat

I began the race genuinely thinking I would be home in a boat, so to speak. Unfortunately, I ended it doing just that, a harbour shuttle whisking me across to the paddock after I had been forced to abandon my damaged car on the far side of the track. It had been one or those races; a day of wildly fluctuating fortunes. A typical Monaco Grand Prix, you could say.

The warm-up on race morning had been dry and the car felt good. Nobody took much notice of me because I was tenth fastest and seemingly not a threat. But there was more to it than that; I knew the potential was there.

Early in the session, I had been as quick as Michael before making changes to my car. That decision turned out to be a mistake but, before we could go back to the original settings, there was a problem with my engine, which ruled out further running. Nonetheless, I had done enough to feel much happier with the car. It was driveable thanks to getting rid of the understeer which had bothered me during qualifying.

I had been annoyed about that on Saturday because, during morning practice, I had been quite quick. I had done a 1.22.6 lap on old tyres and Michael's best had been a 1.22.0 on new tyres. Damon Hill had recorded a 1.21.5 on new tyres and I felt sure I could equal that. I genuinely thought I was in with a chance.

I had kept my new tyres until qualifying, but then we failed to take the weather into account. Usually at a Grand Prix, the temperature rises between the morning session on Saturday and qualifying in the afternoon. At Monaco, the temperature stayed the same and we failed to react quickly enough. The effect on the car with new tyres was crippling understeer. We made a small change to the set up, but it was not enough and the handling problem remained. I had to accept seventh place on the grid. Now, during the early stages of the warm-up on race morning, the car had felt good once again. I was confident. Unfortunately, motor racing is not as simple as that and pendulum was about to swing the other way once more.

Between the end of the warm-up and the approach of the race, it started to rain very hard. This was the first break in the weather all weekend and the rules cater for such an eventuality by allowing drivers to take part in a fifteen-minute acclimatisation session before the start of the race. It is an important move because it gives drivers the chance to learn about the conditions before launching into a wet race. Unfortunately for me, the team was busy changing the engine on my car, so I was unable to take part.

That was a major set-back. With the track being so wet, we were effectively starting from scratch when it came to discovering how fast I could go without flying off the road. During a race, you obviously can't push and hope to get away with a half-spin as you discover the limits of adhesion. There was no alternative but to literally feel my way round the circuit.

When planning our tactics, we tied ourselves in a bit of a knot. With the weather being uncertain for the duration of the race, we decided to go for one stop, but to carry more fuel than usual. They way, if it rained throughout the race, I might be able to run non-stop because, of course, the engine is not being worked so hard in the wet, slippery conditions and therefore uses less fuel. We got so involved with that line of thinking that we failed to stand back and realise that, even if we had known for certain that it was going to be wet all the way, the best option would still have been to stop once. But, because we were so busy trying to be clever and work out the quantity of fuel needed to go all the way in case that happened, we forgot how much I was going to be handicapped by the extra weight.

I went to the grid with a lot of fuel on board, made a good start, found myself in fourth place and pulling away from Barrichello's

Jordan. I was then able to hang on to Gerhard Berger's Benetton in third place. Not a bad position to be in considering overtaking is almost impossible on such a narrow circuit. I remember thinking: 'This is easy'. I should have known better!

All of a sudden, the grip disappeared, possibly due to the tyre temperatures having dropped because I was unable to go quickly enough. It was not difficult to hold up the cars behind. But the guys in front just disappeared into the distance. Even so, I was pleased to be fourth. At that stage, I didn't think I would have to make a pit stop. I was looking reasonably good. I thought Alesi, who was second, would probably hit something or somebody and fail to finish; I thought there was every chance that Hill's leading Williams might break down; and, of course, Michael had put himself out of the race on the first lap by hitting the barrier. My sense of optimism grew even stronger. I remember thinking: 'I can win this'.

I had Heinz-Harald Frentzen behind me and I knew he would not be a problem. Frentzen is a quick driver but, instead of staying calm and working out a means of overtaking me, he acted like a clown. He was darting and weaving in my mirrors, so much so that I knew he was either going to hit the barrier or he was going to hit me. I began to allow margins while braking for the corners so that I could at least make an attempt at getting out of the way while he had his inevitable accident. Despite my precautions, however, Frentzen eventually hit me during a do-or-die mission which was never on from the moment he launched himself at a space that was half the size of his Sauber.

He forced me to run wide but I managed to stay away from the barrier and keep going. I thought: 'That's good. Now he's out of the way'. Once I was free of the Sauber, I was able to concentrate on doing a better job all round. Before the start, Michael had told me to drive off the racing line, because that's where the grip would be when the road was wet. The racing line itself would have too much rubber and would be too slick so, during the early stages at least, I was able to go off line because that also had the bonus of blocking Frentzen as he tried to get by.

However, as the Grand Prix went on, the cars had been gradually drying the racing line and this was working against me now because, of course, Frentzen was right on my tail. I couldn't experiment by trying the outside line. I would have needed to brake a lot earlier in order to discover exactly where the grip was and, given half a chance, Frentzen would have been down the inside and away. I know it sounds Irish, but Heinz-Harald had actually been holding me up quite a lot even though he had been running behind me!

By this stage, there was indeed a lot more grip on the racing line. With the place to myself for a moment or two, I was able to pull away from David Coulthard and the next question – probably the most important of the race – concerned just when to stop and change from wet tyres to slicks. The only thing clear in my mind was that I didn't want to be the first to do it. I reckoned that, since Alesi is one of the best when running on slicks on a wet track, I would wait and see if he made the change and then check his lap time. I used the radio to tell the team to monitor the situation. It would be just as much their decision as it would be mine.

Frentzen was the first driver to make the change and, by checking the split times on his first lap out of the pits, the team could see that he was something like two seconds faster than anyone had been before. It was blindingly obvious what we had to do.

The team called me in straight away, which was a great decision. My pit stop was quick because I was already carrying a lot of fuel on board, which meant very little time was lost refuelling. I rejoined in a comfortable third position. There was no-one close behind me and, at this point, I made a tactical error. Instead of really pushing hard, I thought I would consolidate my position. My tyre pressures were a bit low and, because the track was cold, not enough heat was generated in the tyres to raise the pressures. The whole thing became self-defeating because that meant I couldn't drive hard – and therefore increase the temperatures and pressures.

The next thing I knew was that Olivier Panis was catching me – and everyone else – at the incredible rate of two seconds a lap. The Ligier was absolutely flying; Panis was taking no prisoners. He came up behind me – and just pushed me out of the way as we went round the hairpin outside the Loews Hotel. I suddenly found myself jammed against the barrier. That made it two races out of three (in Germany, if you remember, Panis punted me off at the chicane, the only good thing being that I was on my way to the pits at the time, so it didn't matter) and, as I sat on the outside of the hairpin with my engine stalled, I couldn't help but feel that I owed him one.

I couldn't move and it was obvious that the marshals would need to pull me backwards – which would lead to instant disqualification. The rules say that, as soon as a marshal touches your car then, even if you subsequently restart your car, you are out of the race.

I tried to figure out how they would remove the Ferrari. I felt pretty sure they would use a crane to lift the car out of the way, so I undid my seat belts in order to make a quick exit. The one thing about the marshals at Monaco is that they don't mess about. With a car parked in a dangerous position on such a narrow track, there is no time to lose. If you are not quick about it, they will have the car dangling on the end of a hook before you are out of the cockpit. Shades of my cousin Stephen swinging Derek around the scrapyard all those years ago...

Suddenly, I felt the car being pulled backwards. Then I was able to roll forwards and trickle down the hill. I started the engine by flicking a little switch which engaged the clutch. The engine fired, and off I went. Immediately, I was on the radio, shouting 'Belts! Belts!' as a warning of what to expect when I came into the pits.

The team had been watching the television pictures of the incident and they felt sure I must have smashed the nose of the car. It was a fair assumption to make considering the way I had been unceremoniously parked against the barrier but, in actual fact, the car was not damaged. Everything was fine. Except for my seat harness. If I could have fastened the central buckle, I would have done so. But the cramped confines of the cockpit in a Formula 1 car mean that is an impossible task (when wearing a helmet, the driver can't even *see* the buckle down there on his midriff) and I had no alternative but to stop at the pits.

On certain circuits, it is very difficult to hear clearly what you are saying over the radio. Monaco is one of the worst in that respect. When the team heard me shouting down the radio, they felt sure I must have been saying 'Nose! Nose!', or something to that effect. It was a reasonable assumption to make. I believe there is a name for that particular type of mental syndrome. It was a common problem during the Gulf War, people hearing only what they *expected* the other party to say, even though they the message was nothing of the sort. I could have said 'rubber duck' and they would have sworn I had said 'new nose'.

So, I arrived in the pits and they were so busy changing the tyres and replacing the nose that no one saw me pointing furiously into the cockpit. That cost me a lot of time. Then, to add insult to injury, I stalled the engine!

I have to admit that, by this stage, I could see no point in carrying on. If I managed to get into the top six, the team which finished behind me would protest my assisted start and I would be kicked out. I was as familiar as anyone else with that particular rule. But, before I had time to think further on the subject, the engine was fired and I was being waved out of the pits. I thought: 'May as well carry on until someone says otherwise'.

I had only just rejoined when who should come up behind me but Panis, the Ligier now running strongly in third place. *My* third place! I did give some serious consideration to doing a half spin and getting in his way. That would have made the score 2–1. Then I thought: 'Wait a minute. Doing something like that to a Frenchman in France will be worth a two-race ban. Eddie Irvine doing it to a Frenchman in France will mean a three to four race ban at the very least.' So I let him through!

I followed the Ligier with the intention of trying to worry him into a mistake. But Panis was really on it that afternoon; he drove a very good race and deserved to win. When I congratulated him afterwards, it would have been nice if he had said: 'Sorry about punting you off'. But he didn't. I made a mental note of that.

In the meantime, I had made a quick refuelling stop. And still no disqualification. With fresh tyres and nothing to lose, I thought I would try to set the fastest lap of the race. I was pushing hard when my right-rear wheel hit the kerb on the inside of the same corner where Michael had gone off about an hour and a half before.

The car spun round and I found myself sitting in the middle of the track, just out of sight on the exit of a blind corner. I was more or less on the racing line – and facing the wrong way. The marshals were waving their yellow warning flags but I didn't want to hang around any longer than necessary. My engine was still running, so I quickly spun the car through 180 degrees to face the right direction. Just as I was thinking that had been a close call, Mika Salo came steaming round the corner and thumped into the back of me. I knew he was having a dice for fourth place with Mika Hakkinen and, sure enough, a few seconds later there was another bang. I thought 'That'll be Hakkinen.'

Waved yellow flags mean 'Slow! Be prepared to stop'. I appreciate that these two were fighting for a place but, when the leading driver sees a yellow flag, the irony is that it actually means he is safe for a moment or two because the rules do not permit overtaking in the area under the control of the yellow flags. In fact, it is actually better if the driver doing the chasing does overtake because it removes the pressure; it means he will be thrown out at the end of the race. As far as I could tell, Hakkinen didn't slow at all; he piled into us at a serious rate of knots. And he got away without punishment.

Not long before, Luca Badoer had been fined $5,000 for colliding with Jacques Villeneuve. Villeneuve had been the second of two cars trying to lap the Forti, Badoer having let the first one through as they braked for Mirabeau corner. But then Badoer had to get round the corner himself and he turned in just as Villeneuve was trying to come through as well. It's an easy mistake to make and yet Badoer was fined while Hakkinen and Salo both got away with effectively ignoring a waved yellow flag – a far more serious offence in my book. I don't want to think about what might have happened had I been climbing out of the car at the time.

My more immediate concern was getting back to the paddock before the track was opened to the public and the place became a zoo. There was quite a collection of drivers hanging around Portier Corner looking for a lift. Badoer had eventually come to a stop down there and, of course, the two Mikas and I were on foot after our particular incident. It soon became obvious that the officials had not sent anyone to pick us up, so we hitched a ride on the back of a truck, which took us down to the quayside where we then jumped on board a shuttle boat.

The ride back to the paddock was pretty jovial. Despite our various problems, I think everyone was glad that a hard but boring race was over. Certainly, Salo and Hakkinen were not as upset as you might imagine. They were classified fifth and sixth thanks to there being just four cars running at the finish. Picking up points after driving into each other five laps from the end; you don't get much luckier than that.

I was classified seventh, a poor reward, I felt, at the end of a race which, at times, had promised much. At least I had plenty to talk about that night. For once, there was no hurry to get home. We went to a party at Jimmy's night club and then moved on to the Stars and Bars which had been jumping from the moment the mechanics had finished packing up and moved across to the pub for a drink. It was a great night.

As I explained earlier, Formula 1 people do not often get the chance to socialise together and let their hair down but this was a rare opportunity and everyone seemed intent on making the most of it. It took me back a few years and reminded me of the times spent in Japan while doing Formula 3000. Those were the days when the fun was interrupted by the racing rather than the other way round.

CHAPTER 10

Orient Excess

Taking a step backwards in motor sport is a risky business. Having worked your backside off to move out of one Formula and step onto the next level, there seems little point in sticking your career in reverse a year later, even for just one race. In fact, that makes it worse in a way because, if you get beaten, then people will remember that regardless of how valid your excuse may be on the day. You are expected to win. Period.

Of course, if you can step back and dominate, then the move can give your career the jolt it needs after a disappointing year. You are effectively saying: 'Told you so! I'm as quick as ever. The lack of results recently has had little to do with my driving.' And it's good for the morale to get onto the podium once again after a season spent struggling. But there is the element of risk.

I had to face exactly that sort of decision at the end of my first pretty average year in Formula 3000 in 1989. I was invited to take part in the Formula 3 Macau Grand Prix. My first visit – at the end of 1988 – had created a good impression even though I didn't win. Going back would be very, very difficult. But I said yes.

Once again, I was driving a Theodore Racing entry run by Dick Bennetts. I had a touch of the 'flu, the car wasn't that good either and I just did not feel comfortable all weekend. I could only manage seventh on the grid but I felt I could maybe do something in the race, provided everyone managed to get through the very tight first corner without incident.

I made a good start and was holding fourth as the pack arrived at the corner. The driver on pole position, Otto Rensing, was unchallenged going in but he got it all wrong coming out. His Reynard ended up broadside across the track. The first five cars were taken out on the spot as we had nowhere to go and crashed into each other. That was that.

I was in a similar predicament when asked to do the Macau Grand Prix at the end of 1990, the year I had been with Eddie Jordan Racing in Formula 3000. It had been a slightly better season than the previous one, which wasn't saying much, but I also had the memories of Macau twelve months before. In fact, it would work out much better this time and the decision to go would have very important long-term implications.

I finished third and then joined quite a few of the European drivers as they moved to Japan for a race (with good prize money!) at Fuji. It was a very good circuit for Formula 3 thanks to some quick corners and a long straight. Problems during qualifying and the first part of the race meant thirteenth place on the grid for the final but I then had an amazing race. I hauled my way to third place, overtaking cars left, right and centre; it was just like Formula Ford, only quite a bit quicker. I was able to use the long straight to gain a tow from the car in front. I remember passing four cars in one go. They were fighting among themselves and I was able to tuck into the slipstream of one car, allow that to pull me along and make a sling-shot overtaking move into the slipstream of the next car. And so on. I simply towed my way past the lot of them. Finishing third that day was a brilliant result.

Looking back, it's interesting to note that the races at Macau and Fuji were won by Michael Schumacher. If you had told me then that we would both be driving for Ferrari in 1996, I might have asked you to go for a lie down in a darkened room. I know anything is possible in motor racing but, at that point, my future was uncertain. And, as for Michael, he was obviously considered to be pretty quick and yet he had surprised a lot of people by deciding to go off and race World Championship sportscars for Mercedes-Benz in 1991.

You never know what is in the air. The issue of *Autosport* magazine which ran the report of the race at Fuji also carried pictures of the very first Jordan Formula 1 car, which had been unveiled that week. Our paths would cross in Japan three years later but, in the meantime, my career was about to take a semi-permanent turn to the East.

I had received a couple of offers for another season of Formula 3000 in Europe, but I wasn't keen. What was the point? And yet, the alternatives were few and far between. Then I was asked by the Cerumo team if I was interested in racing in Japan. When they said how much they would pay, the Japanese 3000 series suddenly seemed a very attractive alternative! At the same time, I had an approach from the Nova team, who were also racing in Japanese 3000. They were offering considerably less. So I chose Cerumo. Not long after, it seemed that had been a silly thing to do.

I didn't realise that the tyre situation in Japanese 3000 was so critical. Cerumo ran with Yokohama rubber and I didn't know that Bridgestones (as raced by Nova) were the tyres to have. On the other hand, I was lucky because Nova were distributors for Lola cars and, as such, they were obliged to race the latest model. The 1991 Lola F3000 car would turn out to be a piece of junk. At Cerumo, I could continue with the previous year's Lola. I actually won a race, mainly because it was wet and the disadvantage of running on Yokohama tyres was not so pronounced. In the dry, we had no chance but, having said that, Cerumo was an excellent team and we were the best Yokohama runner by miles. That was the best I could hope for.

We switched to Dunlop for 1992 and fared little better. Instead of finishing seventh in the championship, I finished eighth! It was obvious that we needed to have Bridgestones but, try as they might, the team could not do a deal. Politics of some description were involved and the future was looking so bleak that the team's sponsor, Cosmo Oil, was thinking seriously about pulling out. Then we turned things round quite dramatically.

During a test session at the end of the year, we had Dunlop make a major change to the construction of their tyres. It simply transformed the race rubber. Dunlop's qualifying tyres had always been good – I had claimed four pole positions in nine races – but their race tyres dropped off in performance much too quickly. The change in construction made a massive difference to the race tyres. I had absolutely no doubt that this was the answer.

Cosmo Oil stayed on board and I finished second in the 1993 championship. I would have won it quite easily but for breaking first gear a couple of times at the start and then suffering an engine misfire while leading the race at Sugo. Looking back now, I can see that I was fortunate in my choice to drive with Cerumo. Had I allowed myself to study form, I would probably have chosen Nova and the end result would not have been as satisfying. There has to be a moral in there somewhere.

All in all, life in Japan was excellent even though it hadn't started off that well. At first, I had stayed in a fairly rough hotel simply because it was near the team manager's house in the Shinjuku district of Tokyo. The European drivers tended to use the President Hotel, which was much more up-market. Eventually I moved in there. And that's when the fun really started.

It was a brilliant situation. I was regarded as one of the top drivers, which meant I could ask my price: it was good of Cerumo to pay it! The prize money was serious, too; it was not uncommon to earn US$100,000 for winning a race.

So, here was a bunch of young racing drivers, all earning good money and living in a cosmopolitan city. It was a gas. Drivers came and went each year, of course, but I found myself keeping company with Roland Ratzenberger and the Scandinavians, Eje Elgh and Mika Salo. Johnny Herbert was there for a while. Heinz-Harald Frentzen would hang out with us, as would the Italian driver, Mauro Martini. However, I spent most of my time with the Californian driver, Jeff Krosnoff. He was good fun; a happy-go-lucky character who enjoyed life and yet worked hard at trying to make his name.

You can imagine the banter in the likely event of a driver finding himself in female company at the end of the evening. The hotel would insist on us taking a double room if we returned with a guest. That added another US$50 to the bill, so the trick was to sneak into a single room. The management caught me one night – a phone call to the room said they were on to me even though they could do very little about it at that stage. The following night, I returned with another girl – she was really beautiful, half French, half Japanese – and the night manager saw me. He tried to throw a spanner in the works by coming straight over and saying: 'Last night, you had *another* girl in your room! You can't do this!' Naturally, that caused a bit of consternation in certain quarters! But I got away with it.

Of course, that sort of thing would be a topic of conversation when we met the next evening. The whole thing was like a non-stop party. We would go to the Hard Rock Café and then on to clubs such as the Lexington Queen and Motown. The guy who ran the Lexington Queen was a big fan of motor racing. He would let us in for nothing, supply free drinks and introduce us to the right people. You couldn't go wrong! It was like being on holiday with plenty of money in your pocket, staying in a comfortable hotel, going out every night and having a good time. The only driver who didn't fit in with the gang was Ross Cheever, brother of the former Grand Prix driver, Eddie Cheever. Ross was a loner, a bit of a strange guy. I never managed to work him out.

It was while in Japan that I was introduced to the Le Mans 24-Hour race. Through my contacts, I was offered the drive by Toyota and, to be honest, I did it purely for the money at first. I went to Le Mans hoping that the car would break down. I came away in love with the place.

To my mind, this was a proper motor race, a fast, gutsy event which had everything. Compared to Le Mans, Formula 1, in my opinion anyway, is a bit limp. Le Mans effectively lasts for a week by the time you have signed on, practised during the day and at night, and generally prepared for this marathon. The atmosphere is terrific. At the time, I thought the sight of those out-and-out sports cars was mind-blowing. They proved to be too expensive to build and run, which is why the formula has changed in recent years, but they were awesome cars.

This is a race you can really get your teeth into. People talk about pacing yourself and bringing the car home. That's rubbish. It's flat out all the way. Okay, there will be the odd occasion when the driver is unable to push as hard as he would like. I have raced there three times and, each year, I had one weak stint when I was mentally drained; I was maybe 1.5 seconds per lap slower than normal. Then I would get my second wind and away I would go.

Even if you are two laps behind, it is still possible to win. In 1994, I was sharing a Toyota with Jeff Krosnoff and Mauro Martini. We led most of the way and we were something like a lap and a half ahead with ninety minutes to go. Then the gear lever broke. Jeff was driving and he managed to bring the car back to the pits. The gear lever was fixed and I jumped on board for the final stint. We had dropped to third but, on the last corner of the last lap, I took second place from the Porsche of Thierry Boutsen. We would have won easily – which would have been very nice – but to finish second under circumstances like that was just fantastic. To snatch second place at the last corner after twenty-four hours of racing was a brilliant feeling. I could hear the crowd. That sort of thing doesn't happen very often in Formula 1. Certainly, the way things were going with Ferrari, I knew I was unlikely to experience anything similar during the seventh round of the 1996 championship in Spain.

Having said that, things had been looking up. I had actually been allowed *two* days of testing! After having spent so long without any useful running, the test at Mugello was really nice. We worked our way through a number of different options on the set up of the car and learned quite a lot. The problem was, of course, that we didn't have any quick fixes. But, for me, it was a pleasure to be able to work through things logically and without any pressure on time. I had an eight-hour day and, to make it complete, the weather was beautiful. Tuscany is a gorgeous part of the world, a bit like a sunny Ireland, and the Mugello track is excellent. It is a good place to go testing, the only problem being that, on a hot day, the tyres are put through hell. That makes it expensive because, in order to keep a baseline when experimenting with various things, the tyres always need to be at the same level. So, when it's hot and the level of grip drops dramatically, you need to keep putting fresh tyres on the car.

From my point of view, the work done during the test had allowed me to learn about the car and I felt a lot more confident going to Barcelona for the Grand Prix. I qualified sixth – and felt it should have been fifth but for Gerhard Berger's Benetton pipping me right at the end. Michael had put his Ferrari on the second row, just 0.75 seconds ahead of me, so I was quite happy.

In fact, everything was working out well. The hotel chosen by the Ferrari team did not amount to much but it had the advantage of being located on a quiet hillside, just five minutes from the circuit. When I was with Jordan, we stayed in the next best thing to a transport cafe with motorways either side. It was impossible to get a decent night's sleep. This time, there was no such problem even though we were cut off from the social scene. Not that it made any difference to me.

It was the usual scenario. By the time I had finished debriefing and doing interviews, it was 7 pm. When I returned to the hotel an hour later, I couldn't be bothered going out. It was a case of taking a shower, ordering dinner, eating in my room and then settling down with a book.

While in Spain I was studying a manual on flying helicopters. I had previously abandoned any idea of a helicopter, particularly after joining Ferrari, the hectic schedule having limited my flying time to three hours in six months. The original plan, formulated when I thought I would be with Jordan in 1996, was to fly back and forth between Dublin and the Jordan factory at Silverstone. I reckoned I could leave my back garden and be at Silverstone in two hours.

I had started taking flying lessons. I make a point of only learning things which are useful. With the exception of something like water skiing, I'm not into doing things just for fun. Helicopters are serious money and, at the time, I thought it was worthwhile. Then, with the move to Ferrari, there seemed little point in carrying on because, obviously, Italy is too difficult to reach by helicopter. It would take something like fifteen hours to get there. However, having gone so far with the flying lessons, I was determined to find time in order to win my licence.

I had been working with Phoenix Helicopters, a company based to the west of Dublin. It had been very difficult initially, very tiring, but having got through that stage, it seemed silly to abandon the idea even though the original plan had been completely changed by my move to Ferrari.

To be honest, having a helicopter would be a nice toy. I couldn't see the point in earning money and saving it when all I wanted was a few gardening tools and enough cash to buy some flowers. The more I thought about it, the more I liked the idea of owning a nice helicopter. Hence the reading material in Spain. The book covered aviation rules and the laws of aerodynamics, most of which I knew anyway thanks to my school days and subsequent experience working with racing cars.

On the night before the race, I had received a call from a friend in Madrid who said it was pouring with rain there. When I finished reading and closed the curtains, it was the end of a beautiful day in Barcelona. I thought no more about it.

The following morning, it was some time before I happened to look out of the window. When I did, I had a complete shock. The rain was pelting down and it looked set for the rest of the day. That would turn the Spanish Grand Prix on its head.

The first clue about our competitiveness in the wet would come during the thirty-minute warm-up. I was fifth fastest which, on paper, did not look too bad. But, deep down, I was not particularly happy with the car; I didn't feel comfortable and, with no sign of any let-up in the rain, I wasn't as confident as I would have liked. Then, a few seconds into the race, I thought I was looking good!

I had made a reasonable getaway and tucked into fifth place, just behind Berger, who seemed quite slow. But I didn't want to take any chances, particularly as Michael had made a bad start and was somewhere in the spray behind me. Above all else, I had to keep an eye on him. I knew Michael was going to be pretty quick in the race (he had been over a second quicker than me during the warm-up) and the last thing I wanted to do was turn in to a corner and find him alongside. It was almost impossible to see where he was. Certainly, as we finished the first lap, he did not seem to be making any attempt to come through.

The next thing I knew, I was spinning off the track. Just like that. I don't know what caused it. It could have been a puddle but, in truth, I have no idea. All of a sudden I was off the road and spinning very quickly across the slippery grass. When I finally came to a halt, the nose of the car was up against a tyre barrier. I tried to do a three-point turn but only succeeded into reversing into a big dip in the ground, where the car became well and truly stranded. That was that. I climbed out and got soaked walking back to the pits.

I was, to put it mildly, pretty hacked off, particularly when I could see the fantastic job Michael was doing. By lap five, he was in third place; by lap twelve, he was in the lead. We had chosen to put a full wet set-up on our cars (Damon Hill had, for some reason, gone for an intermediate set up in the forlorn hope that the track would dry) and opted to stop twice, unlike the majority who had decided to stop just once. We had clearly chosen the perfect tactic and I couldn't help but think that Ferrari would have enjoyed a one-two finish had I not left the road.

I changed into my civvies and watched the rest of the race on the television in the motorhome because I didn't want to get in the team's way. Michael drove a brilliant race. The win removed a lot of the pressure from him and the team and, even though the victory came in unusual circumstances, it was a win nonetheless. The whole crew was ecstatic because, with Hill having spun off, the championship was alive once more.

I stayed around for a while after the race had finished, and then headed for the airport. I was very pleased for the team, but, to be honest, I didn't feel there was much for me to celebrate. I hadn't done anything to help achieve such a welcome result. In fact, I should have stayed and savoured the atmosphere for a bit longer. Ferrari's fortunes were about to crash in a big way.

CHAPTER 11

A Bloody Nose

Each time I go to Canada for the Grand Prix, I can't help but think I ought to become a photographer or a journalist. Talk about an easy life. Photographers just push a button, hand the film to someone else and then head for the nightclubs. All I hear from the media the following day is talk of the strip joints and the beautiful girls. That can be difficult to take when you have spent most of the previous evening sifting through the telemetry and studying figures of a different kind. Montreal turned out to be the usual story. I got as far as the Hard Rock Café on the first evening. And that was it. Mind you, we did have a lot to talk about inside the team.

The mood was definitely upbeat. The invigorating effect of the Spanish result two weeks before still lingered and we had been carrying out useful development work with revisions to the car, the most noticeable being a high nose which changed the appearance of the F310 quite dramatically. I wasn't bothered about how it looked; in my view, the new nose was a good move simply because it worked.

Michael had tested the nose at Imola and said he didn't like it. Further changes were made and I was summoned to try the next version at Mugello. Straightaway, I could tell that this was an improvement over the original low-mounted version. I don't know why Michael found very little difference between the old and the new; perhaps it is because sensitivity in a car is not such a big problem for him. But, for me, the new nose was definitely a useful development.

As I said before, making the tyres last at Mugello can be a

problem. With the low nose, the tyres would begin to lose their edge after a couple of laps. There were no signs of that when running the high nose. We did back-to-back comparisons and there was no doubt that the latest version was much better. The car felt more progressive when turning into the corners and it didn't understeer on the way out. We were also trying other bits and pieces but the revised nose was the most important change. For once, I really enjoyed driving the car. Plans were rushed through to have the revisions ready for both cars in time for Canada. We were going to Montreal with a high nose and high hopes.

In fact, I didn't have the high nose until the second day of practice. The truth is, however, that it did not make a massive amount of difference on that particular track and, in any case, I was making changes (unsuccessfully, as it would turn out) to the car between qualifying runs and I failed to get the best out of my tyres when they were brand new. Even so, Michael was third on the grid and I was less than half a second behind in fifth place. I had been close to Michael in terms of lap times throughout practice and, even though he had got his act together a bit better than me during qualifying, I was reasonably happy. I was ahead of Gerhard Berger's Benetton and Mika Hakkinen's McLaren. Things appeared to be moving in the right direction.

I was more concerned about the growing amount of pain in my back. Increasing the arch in the seat did not help and we eventually worked out that the problem was being caused by the fact that I had been doing so little mileage in the car. The act of hitting the brake pedal in a racing car brings certain back muscles into play and they had not been used very much in recent months.

The problem was made worse when I did finally go testing because Mugello does not call for heavy braking. But I soon knew all about it at Montreal. The circuit is more or less made up of a number of chicanes joined by short straights. That means heavy acceleration and very hard braking: it's stop-go, stop-go. The Circuit Gilles Villeneuve was exposing the fact that I was not fully race fit. The way things would work out over the next few races, fitness would be the least of my problems.

Confirmation that I had not been getting the most out of the car while running new tyres came during the warm-up on race morning. The car felt great on old tyres. Everything came together and I genuinely felt that this was going to be a good race for me, provided I could make a decent start.

Since it continued to be difficult to know exactly when the clutch was going to bite, the only way to make a half-decent getaway was to keep my right foot flat to the floor and let the clutch out with a bang as soon as the starting lights went out. The drawback is a lot of wheel spin – and that's what happened in Montreal. Luckily enough, everyone behind me made bad starts as well. The cars in front managed to pull away but the important point was that no one had overtaken me as we left the grid.

By this stage, my troubles were minor when compared to the problems experienced by Michael. His engine had refused to start and, by the time they got it going, the field had left the grid for the final parade lap. The rules do not permit a driver to return to his proper grid position. Michael had no choice but to start from the back. Straightaway I had gained a place, even if it was at the expense of my team-mate.

I was fourth, hard on Alesi's tail. I thought about having a go at the Benetton but, since this was Alesi, I decided it was best not to risk anything. I needed to finish the race after the disaster in Spain. At the start of the second lap, I was settling into a comfortable fourth place when the front of the car suddenly hit the deck. Part of the front suspension – the pushrod on the right-hand side – had snapped. It was totally unexpected and we never did find out why such an unusual failure had occurred. We assumed the pushrod had been hit by a bolt or some similar object lying on the track. I got out of everyone's way and then returned slowly to the pits. I knew my race was over. Michael's lasted until two-thirds distance, a drive shaft failing as he accelerated away from a pit stop. Damon Hill and Jacques Villeneuve gave Williams their third one-two of the season, Hill opening up a healthy lead in the Championship.

I had a very pleasant diversion on my way from the track to Montreal airport. A friend of mine, Denis Lacroix, works for Bell

Helicopters and he arranged to pick me up and let me fly their latest model, the 407. It was an absolute gem; a stunning piece of kit. We flew to Bell's Canadian headquarters, where I had a look around, and then they dropped me at the airport. On the flight home I worked out the costs. I have to admit that I was sorely tempted but when I looked closely at the figures, US$1.5 million for my first helicopter seemed a bit excessive! It didn't make sense. People would think I was barking mad. But I don't think the man from Bell realised how close he had been to a sale as we zoomed along at 140 knots. It was so impressive.

I walked into the Dalkey Island Hotel at 10.30 am on Monday and caught everyone by surprise; they had just finished watching the highlights of the Canadian Grand Prix on television and there I was, back home and raring to go on my jet-ski. I had been the owner of the Yamaha ski for almost a year and yet I had never had the chance to use it. For once the weather was perfect and I didn't want to waste a moment.

It's a stand-up jet-ski. It's very fast but, because of my inexperience, I found it very difficult to handle, particularly in the rough sea. Of course, I was going at it like a bull in a china shop, trying to run before I could walk. I gave myself a few bruises on the shins but, once I was up and running, it was an exhilarating experience. There is nothing in my racing contract which forbids such activity although, if I looked carefully, I might find a clause in my insurance. But I would rather not know about that; my philosophy is that you've got to live.

During the free weekend between Canada and the French Grand Prix, I demonstrated a Ferrari – and I broke it by trying to treat the car like a dragster! For the past couple of years, the Earl of March had been successfully promoting a Festival of Speed at Goodwood in Sussex. This had grown into quite a social event and he had asked Luca di Montezemolo if he would send a car for the 1996 event. The Ferrari president though it would be the right thing to do since the British have always been keen supporters, and customers, of Ferrari. I was only too pleased to be asked to do the driving. I thought it would be a fun weekend.

They picked me up in Dublin and flew me over in a private plane for what turned out to be a lovely garden party. But, as for the so-called course we were supposed to use ... Set out on narrow driveways in the grounds of Goodwood House, it was less than ideal if you were at the wheel of a 700 bhp Grand Prix car.

The Earl of March has done an amazing job of selling the event. It is a great occasion; an excuse for people to meet. At the end of the day, that's all motoring enthusiasts need. They simply want to look at the cars. It's not necessary, in my opinion, to run them. When I was not so cynical about this business, I used to be satisfied with simply looking at a parked Ferrari or whatever. If I heard there was a Lotus 7 in the neighbourhood, I would go out of my way to see it.

Ferrari had sent one of the 1995 cars. I had no intention of going quickly all the way up the course because of its inadequacies. I thought I would do tyre-smoking burnouts, just to get the crowd going. I did that – and a drive shaft broke. I don't think any Formula 1 car could have withstood that sort of punishment!

It was a two-day affair and I stayed overnight in Goodwood House. I was invited to a Black Tie party that night but, as I was a guest, I had a good excuse not to wear a dinner jacket. I hate dressing up. Some people would feel uncomfortable wearing trousers and a shirt when everyone else is decked out in their finery. But I felt wonderfully at home; it didn't bother me at all. I sat with the Earl of March's sister, Lily, who was great company, a very amusing dinner companion. The seating had been cleverly planned because Lily turned out to be a counsellor and she spent most of the night quietly analysing me – or trying to. I think I was beyond her capabilities.

I had a similar feeling about my car as soon as I completed just a few laps on the first day of practice for the French Grand Prix. I knew immediately that I would be in trouble with the Magny-Cours track. It is amazing how quickly I can tell. In Canada, the car felt good. In France, it felt bad. Simple as that. I knew that, whatever we did to the car, it wouldn't be enough to get us onto the pace which we had hoped for. We worked and worked and worked, but the car was not competitive at any stage in France.

Michael put his car on pole position – how, I will never know. I put it down to Michael having a more intimate knowledge of a car which he had spent the year so far developing. It had to suit him a lot better than it suited me. I qualified in tenth place, but all of that would soon prove to be irrelevant.

During practice, my car had been selected for a random technical check. The officials measured the dimensions of the car, including the so-called turning vanes or air deflectors fitted alongside the front wheels. When the deflectors were found to be 15 mm outside the permitted size, the car was declared illegal and my times were disallowed. I would be forced to start from the back of the grid. To be honest, I wasn't particularly annoyed about that. From tenth place to twenty-second made little difference. Had I been in the top five, I would have been pretty upset. But, in this case, I knew it would not take long to fight my way back to tenth place.

At no stage in my career had I started from the back of a grid. This would be a new experience. I knew I would overtake a few people and have fun. In some ways, it is a nice feeling to be sitting at the back with absolutely nothing to lose and surrounded by drivers in poor cars. They would be half-expecting me to come through.

This was also an unusual situation in that one Ferrari was on pole position and the other was at the very back. But not for long. When we set off on the final parade lap, I saw a red car parked on the grass. At first I though it must be one of the Arrows but, when I saw both of the Arrows drivers not far ahead of me, I realised the worst. Michael was out of the race before it had even started. His engine had blown. I remember thinking: 'My God. There's going to be a big stink about this. The Italian press will have a field day. Irvine illegal on Saturday and Schumacher breaks down on the warm-up.' Now it was down to me to produce.

As a result of the problems we had been having at the start of the previous races, Ferrari had switched to a different type of clutch. It worked perfectly and I made a great start, one of the best I have ever made in Formula 1. I overtook five cars but then I had to back off because a mid-field bunch had made poor getaways and there was no room for me to go through.

I made up more ground during the next few laps. I had just taken fifteenth place when the gearbox hydraulics began to play up. Each time I tried to select a gear, it would pop into neutral. This was while changing down going into the hairpin. Suddenly I was free-wheeling and I nearly went off the road. I thought: 'That's all they need to see: me flying off the road after starting from the back of the grid. They wouldn't be impressed.'

The gearbox re-engaged. I managed to stop the car, take the corner and get going again. Then the same thing happened not long after. There was nothing for it but to cruise back to the pits and end a desperate day for Ferrari.

The mood could best be described as quiet. Even with the background noise from the race, the absence of conversation in the garage was noticeable. I felt so sorry for Jean Todt. He had worked so hard, but there was only so much he could do. It wasn't the end of the world. The team was down, but not depressed.

A mechanical failure is not a crime but, the following morning, the Italian press made it a capital offence. That was bad. The situation had not been helped by the Italian team doing badly in the Euro '96 football competition. Now the journalists were calling for Jean's resignation. That was too ridiculous for words. Just four weeks before, we were full of hope, what with the win in Spain and useful modifications to the front of the car. Now all we had to show for it was a bloody nose.

CHAPTER 12

Real Bad News

If I thought the F310 was bad in France, I was in for a shock at Silverstone. I have never driven anything which felt so difficult to handle. In fact, it was frightening. I simply could not understand why a racing car should be like that. The team had completed many hours of testing and yet we arrived at the scene of the tenth round of the championship with a car which was nervous and totally unpredictable.

On my second lap of practice, I spun at Bridge Bend. That's no place to lose control, believe me. Bridge is a very fast right-hander taken at about 160 mph. I wasn't pushing particularly hard but, suddenly, the car was gone. I thought I was going to hit the wall but I came off the brakes and just managed to steer away from the concrete. It was a close call.

Throughout the two days of practice, it was a matter of trying to keep up with the car. I can honestly say that I didn't know what it was going to do next. Point the Ferrari at the apex of a corner and sometimes it would get there, sometimes not. It might try to go straight on; on other occasions it would snap into oversteer. I was having to drive the car every metre of the way rather than letting it flow. In the end, I was only one second off Michael's pole-position time after wringing the car's neck for one banzai lap. But the fact that I was tenth on the grid after all that effort said everything.

I had prepared for the British Grand Prix knowing that it was going to be tough. The circuit would be fast and very bumpy, none of which would suit the Ferrari. On top of that, the British based teams had been running continually at Silverstone because this is their designated test track. Ferrari had nominated Monza, so our advantage would come there but, in the meantime, I was not looking forward to this race.

Before the action started at Silverstone, I had been working in London, visiting the Virgin Megastore and doing a talk with Shell. Then I was supposed to meet Michael and Jean Todt at Battersea and travel to Silverstone by helicopter. I arrived late at the heliport to find they had had no alternative but to meet their slot time, leaving me to make the two-hour trip by road. I should have known better than to rely on the record industry to keep to their time schedules.

The problems which followed during practice merely added to the frustration. On a wider scale, I felt there was no way the car should handle the way it did. I had one or two ideas. I talked to Jean Todt and design chief John Barnard and they were sympathetic. The short answer was that the team was under pressure to achieve the results we knew we were capable of and I would have to keep my head down and work as hard as everyone else.

In any case, the mood within the team remained very optimistic and there were lighter moments along the way. On the Thursday afternoon, Shell held a press conference in their suite in the Paddock Club. Jean and I were on stage, with the media and various guests seated in front of us. While everyone was sorting themselves out, I had spotted a very attractive girl in the audience. She had also come to Jean's attention. He leaned across and said: 'Look at the one in row three.' Unfortunately for Jean, he had failed to realise that I was already hooked up to the sound system thanks to a microphone attached to my shirt. His piece of advice was heard by everyone in the room. Including the babe in row three…

It was an amusing moment and Jean saw the funny side. In a way, though, I felt sorry of him because he had enough on his plate without making a slip-up in front of the media. To my mind, he was one of the most important people on the team and he did not deserve the hammering he was receiving from the Italian press. Jean's problem, it seemed to me, was that too much of his time was being spent worrying about details which should have been looked after by someone else. Jean has been working hard, trying to bring the right people to the team. He had the least envious job in the world. I don't know how much he was earning in the middle of 1996 but, given the problems he was having to shoulder at the time, the figure was probably ten times less then it should have been.

Jean was doing a better job than most politicians. Which reminds me, I was introduced to Tony Blair as the leader of the Labour Party did a pit tour with his wife on race morning. Like all politicians, he talked, but said nothing. I can't relate to that way of working. If I'm talking to someone, then that's what I do. If I have nothing to say, I don't waste everyone's time. It seems to me that people in a position of power and importance have a habit of going through the motions of conversation while looking for a photo opportunity. Tony Blair was the same, although his wife seemed very genuine. But then she is not a politician.

During all of this pre-race build-up, everyone had been asking about the prospects for a good result in my home Grand Prix. I told the team that, if I was to have any chance of hanging on to the leaders, I would need to be no lower than seventh at the end of the first lap. If I was stuck further down the field, I would get nowhere.

I was actually quite confident that I could manage that. My only concern was that David Coulthard and Martin Brundle – both good starters – were alongside and directly in front of me on the grid. In the event, I zapped past them both. I was very pleased with myself! In fact, I almost took Barrichello as well going through the first corner. We were side-by-side and then the Jordan-Peugeot had the better line for the run towards Becketts.

I had to be content with seventh and I knew it would remain that way. I was quicker than Rubens but it was impossible to overtake thanks to the cars being closely matched and aerodynamically sensitive when running in close company. As soon as a car got close to the one in front, the leading car would deprive the one following of air to the nose wings. Suddenly, the attacking car would have no downforce at the front. The effect of that would be like hitting a patch of ice; turn the wheel and not much happens. It proved once again that something drastic needed to be done in order to improve the quality of the racing. The British Grand Prix would turn out to be deadly dull as a result. The drivers at the front of the grid simply needed to make a good start and the race would be over. Assuming, of course, that their cars held together.

At the end of the first lap, I was three places behind Michael. When I saw smoke coming from the back of his car, I thought : 'Jeez, here we go again!' I checked my mirrors but my car seemed to be okay. Michael lasted for just one more lap before pulling off with a broken gearbox.

Now I was sixth, still stuck behind Barrichello. Berger was less than a second behind me but I knew he could do little about it. I was happy to wait until the first pit stop because I knew Ferrari would be faster than Jordan, and Rubens tended to be very slow coming in and going out. He would be fairly easy to pick off.

I didn't get that far. Towards the end of lap five, huge plumes of smoke erupted from the back of my car. By the time I got on the radio to say I had a problem, I had passed the entrance to the pit lane. I carried on while waiting to see if either the smoke would stop or the telemetry in the garage could provide any answers. When the smoke continued, I cruised along the side of the track and asked the team for further instructions. I was told to stop at the pits which I did. A bearing in the differential had broken. My race was over. Members of the press were waiting to pounce.

I sat down with Jean Todt and told him exactly what I thought. Jean agreed with me. We both understood what needed doing, but I could see that getting it done would be another matter. It's not that easy. Everyone knows how to win a Formula 1 race but actually achieving the situation which allows it to happen is very difficult. There are so many things involved. It's a complex business.

I had been around long enough to understand that. But I felt I wanted to get this of my chest. Initially, I had thought: 'I'm lucky to be with Ferrari'. At the end of the day, however, I knew I was as good as anyone, with the possible exception of Michael. I wanted to have the chance to prove that, which is why I wanted to become more involved within the team. We were past the half-way stage of the season and I had not done much development work on the car.

That was understandable, but the fact remained that I was not much further on than I had been at the start of the year. I was made aware by Jean that Ferrari understood this.

I had to admit that, in the past, the British Grand Prix had not really meant that much to me over and above any other Grand Prix. But, in 1996, it did seem special. There were a lot of Irish flags in the spectator enclosures and I was aware of people shouting my name. There seemed to be much more support than before.

It can be a double-edged sword, of course. I found that I was unable to stand around and chat as much as I would have liked. The problem is that the fans will not leave the drivers alone and the drivers tend to go to ground as a result. It has always baffled me why people want scraps of paper autographed. But what annoys me is the constant interruptions when I am trying to have a conversation. Maybe it's wrong, but I just don't like signing autographs at such times. I don't mind doing one or two, but when your whole life is spent signing autographs it becomes too much and you tend to want to hide. And then people get upset because they can't see the drivers.

It's a vicious circle, I suppose. The one chance the drivers have to relax at Silverstone is after the race when Jordan hosts a rock party in the paddock. But even that became too much on this occasion. I had been trying to talk with a small group of friends. We were in a circle which I would have thought was enough to convey the message that this was a private conversation. And yet I was continually pushed and prodded by people who wanted things signed. I will never understand how anyone can be that rude. If you stand facing everyone, with your arms open, then the body language is clear. On this occasion, I was huddled with my mates but the message was being ignored. All of that, however, was about to become totally irrelevant.

I was enjoying a quiet beer when Adam Cooper, a British journalist who had covered the Japanese scene when I was there, came down from the press room to say that there had been a big shunt in an Indycar race in Toronto. The accident had involved Jeff Krosnoff. Adam had seen the pictures on Eurosport and he said the car was in bits. It looked very bad. Adam is an experienced observer and he is not prone to exaggeration. I could tell from his manner that it was very serious indeed. Straight away, I had a terrible feeling about the whole thing.

All sorts of images flash through your mind. I recalled that I did not know anyone when I first went to Japan. At my first test, this guy from California had come walking down the pit lane, stuck out his hand and said: 'Hi. How are you? I'm Jeff Krosnoff.' That was the start of it. Jeff would turn out to be the best friend I had in Japan. A more genuine and honest person you couldn't wish to meet. Jeff was liked by everyone; I don't think he had an enemy in the world.

We had shared the second-place Toyota at Le Mans, of course, but our friendship extended beyond work. We had been to Guam together on holiday. I had met his wife and stayed at their place in California; typically, we all got on really well and had a great laugh. His father had visited Japan a couple of times and I had got to meet him, as well as Jeff's mother. Jeff and I had spoken on the phone earlier in the year and I was as pleased as everyone else when he got the Indycar drive. All of that made the news from Toronto even more difficult to take in.

I went round to the back of the motorhome, just to get away from everyone. I was sitting alone, with my head down, when someone appeared and stuck a pen and paper under my nose. I told him to 'F*** off!', which, I admit, wasn't very nice. It wasn't the man's fault; he didn't know the circumstances. But, at that precise moment, I had simply had enough. I wanted to get away from Silverstone. Everyone was having a good time making merry. It was the last thing I felt like doing. I went back to Oxford and the house I was sharing with a couple of friends. The news reports later that night confirmed that Jeff was dead.

How does a driver react under circumstances such as these? In my case, the first thing I want to do is see the accident for myself, not through any mawkish sense, but because the first priority is to determine what caused it. It is a self-protection mechanism of sorts. I want to see what can be learned and to say: 'Well, I wouldn't have done it that way.' Then you begin to feel reassured. Although it appears strange to want to see how a friend was killed, it's an

Above: Still a long way to go for Ferrari … and for me as the pits look a long way off from my unofficial parking spot during practice in Argentina back in April.

Below: A crucial period during the race. Tyres changed, I wait for the refuelling to finish before roaring back into the fray. All in the space of a few seconds.

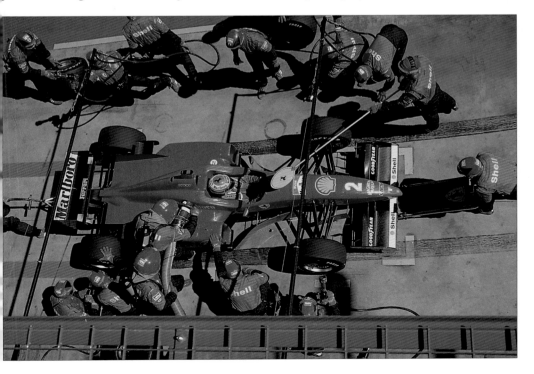

Above: Making the most of a Marlboro trip to the slopes during the winter of 1995/96.

Below: I like this kind of driving when time permits (left). Straining to make a point on the tennis court (right). Just as well I don't do this for a living.

Above: 'I tell you, it's this bad…' Ferrari Sporting Director Jean Todt looks as though he has heard it all before as I discuss the F310.

Below: Spinning out of contention in Germany. The Ligier of Olivier Panis knocked me out of the European Grand Prix at the Nurburgring in April.

Above: 'So, Mr. President, what about the spare parts you promised for my GTO?' Chatting with Ferrari president, Luca di Montezemolo, on the grid at the Nurburgring.

Below: Always a great reception from the Imola crowd – provided they stay in their seats. At the end of the race, it was pandemonium with people pulling and pushing me.

Above: Battling with back trouble at Imola.
After about five laps of the race I had been
in absolute agony, the result of trying a new
seat in the car.

Below: Letting the old boys have their fun.
Niki Lauda, technical advisor to Ferrari,
shares a joke with his former team-mate,
John Watson, during practice at Monaco.

Above: Negotiating the hairpin during an incident-packed race at Monaco. At one stage, I thought I had a chance of winning…

Below: Talking to The Boss. Gianni Agnelli, the President of Fiat, visited the British Grand Prix to see how the Formula 1 division of his empire was getting on.

Michael Schumacher and I received a warm reception from the crowd during the drivers' parade at Silverstone. Unfortunately we had both retired within the first six laps of the race.

Off the road and out of the race with gearbox trouble in Belgium.

Rod Vickery (left), my manager, and John Barnard, Ferrari designer, doubtless discussing the merits of their driver.

Left: At last, some quality time at home. I have an ear for good music – but my friends say this hardly qualifies…

Below: Time on my hands during testing. Waiting at Paul Ricard with my girlfriend Nicola.

Below: It's a tough job, but someone has to do it. My first year with Ferrari proved a testing time … at least things could only improve in 1997.

important part of the healing process. I want to be able to say that the accident could have been avoided by this or by that. At the end of the day, it will always stand you in good stead, particularly if you come across a similar situation. You will be able to say to yourself: 'Back off. You know this can go wrong.'

Jeff's accident was a shock. Sadly, however, it was nothing new for me. I find it hard to take on board the number of drivers I have known personally who have lost their lives during the ten years or so I have been racing. When I was racing Formula Ford in 1987, an English driver, Pete Rogers, was killed at Donington. I had got to know Pete quite well because Quest, the team he drove for, was usually parked quite close to Van Diemen in the paddock. Within the space of a month in 1992, Marcel Albers, a Dutchman I had got to know, and Hitoshi Ogawa, my team-mate in Japanese Formula 3000, were both killed. Then Roland Ratzenberger had a fatal accident during the same weekend Ayrton Senna was killed at Imola.

I couldn't claim to be unaware of the risks associated with the sport and yet people used to suggest I was a bit of a madman on the track. I didn't think that was the case at all. I have always felt I did everything to avoid being involved in dodgy situations. There is a suggestion that the danger element is part of the attraction; 'dicing with death' and 'wow! that was close, but I got away with it.' That's all nonsense. It's not my scene. In fact, as far as I'm concerned, the danger element is the one off-putting fact about motor racing.

You side-step the thought by assuming it is not going to happen to you. And yet, the strange thing is that the drivers I mentioned were not the sort to take big risks. Jeff was passionate about his motor racing but he didn't mix it, and he didn't get involved unnecessarily. It was the same with Ogawa; he never made a risky overtaking manoeuvre in his life. Hitoshi was one of the safest drivers on the track, an Alain Prost, the sort who just did not get involved in anything dubious.

It is difficult to rationalise the spate of incidents involving drivers of that type. Perhaps they were susceptible because they had not come across accidents such as these while racing in the lower Formulae. Maybe they didn't know the situations to avoid. For example, I had an accident very similar to Ogawa's during my first season of motor racing. Another driver was trying to stop me from overtaking. We were both weaving to and fro and eventually he braked for a corner and I went over the top of him. I learned about that sort accident when it was 'safe' to do so. Formula Ford is a good training ground from that point of view. You can make mistakes and come to appreciate what can go wrong without getting hurt. Formula Ford cars are very strong, they don't go particularly fast and they are quite light, which means there is not a lot of energy to be dissipated in the event of an accident. At the end of the day, you have to watch out for dangerous situations. That was why I was keen to find out exactly what had happened to Jeff.

I saw the accident once on television, but it happened so quickly that I could not make head nor tail of it. All I knew was that it had been horrendous and the only consolation was that Jeff probably knew very little about it. I went to bed but couldn't sleep. I got up, watched television for a while and then took two Melatonin, returned to bed and went to sleep immediately. I spent most of Monday trying to wake up, which was a pity because I was playing in a charity golf match in aid of The British Brain and Spine Foundation. The only good thing you could say was that events during the previous twenty-four hours had made the problems at Ferrari seem minor.

CHAPTER 13

A Punishing Schedule

I was ready to fly to California for Jeff Krosnoff's funeral when I learned that I was needed at Fiorano to do a collaudo in preparation for the German Grand Prix. I was very disappointed at not being there to pay my last respects, but at least my father was able to use my ticket and act as my representative. In fact, my mother went to the States as well. They told me it was a very big funeral, with people from all over the world in attendance.

One or way or another, Jeff was in my thoughts. He had been a super-fit guy, a brilliant athlete. When we lived in Tokyo, the drivers would run round the grounds of the Imperial Palace as part of their fitness routine. I don't know how long the run was, but Jeff held the course record of just over 11 minutes; the next best was Mauro Martini with a time of 13 minutes. When Jeff and I went on holiday to Guam, he would be up first thing in the morning. 'Come on Ed!' he'd say. 'Are you up?' (I'd only just come in!) He would set off to do his run and his exercises, return before midday and then we would play some tennis. He had more strength and energy than anyone I've ever known.

As I mentioned earlier, Jeff and I had shared a Toyota at Le Mans and that led me to think about the far-reaching consequences of that weekend. I know Le Mans is not everyone's cup of tea but that race really had been good to me. The Toyota suited me very well. During a stint in the middle of the night in 1993, I was six or seven seconds a lap faster than anyone else.

Eddie Jordan turned up at Le Mans that year. We hadn't really seen much of each other since I had left his Formula 3000 team and moved to Japan. We talked about Formula 1 and Eddie mentioned the possibility of a test drive. Nothing came of it but I was eventually asked if I would be interested in doing the last three races of the Grand Prix season for Jordan. Eddie had been having difficulties finding a decent Number 2 driver that year. Ivan Capelli had lasted for two races and Thierry Boutsen, his replacement, had been a disappointment. Michael Schumacher had made an impressive Formula 1 debut with Jordan in Belgium in August; in fact, it was so good that Benetton snapped up Michael before Eddie knew what was going on! Anyway, Jordan was looking for someone – and had to admit that I was interested.

I spoke to the team I was driving for in the Japanese F3000 series. They said: 'No way'. The last thing they wanted was for me to disappear back to Europe; I was leading the championship and they wanted to win it. Their sponsor, Cosmo, had been trying for three or four years to claim the title and they had never been as close as this. Eventually it was agreed that I could do the last two Grands Prix because they did not clash although, strictly speaking, they could not have stopped me if I had really insisted.

In fact, I was quite ambivalent about the whole Formula 1 situation. I was keen – and yet I wasn't as keen as perhaps I should have been when presented with an opportunity which other drivers would kill for. I would accept the drive for the fun of it all. Then I could say: 'I've done Formula 1.' That was it, really. Since I didn't think EJ would pay me enough money, the plan would be to race in two Grands Prix, enjoy the moment, and then get out.

My first race was at Suzuka in Japan. As soon as the news was announced, it was immediately assumed by the media that I had got the drive because I already knew Suzuka very well. It is one of the longest and most difficult circuits on the Formula 1 calendar and knowledge of the track would be an advantage. To be perfectly honest, I didn't think that was an issue although, looking back, I realise it was probably quite useful. I was very relaxed about the whole thing because, as I said, it would amount to nothing more than a fun experience.

At the end of the first few practice sessions, my name was near the top of the list. I had tried a fresh set of tyres before everyone else and, immediately, I was doing competitive times. I was right up there with the likes of Prost and Senna. It was amazing. Suddenly, the guys from the British press were tripping over each other as they made a rare visit to the Jordan garage. As far as I was concerned, it was not a big deal. I had a right chuckle; I thought it was as funny as hell.

I qualified in eighth place; not bad for a novice! I knew from past experience that it is possible to run round the outside of the first corner at Suzuka and make up places. I made a good start and, as planned, overtook people like Hill and Schumacher on the way through the opening corner. Before I knew it, I was in fifth place! It wouldn't last for long.

The state-of-the-art in car technology in 1993 was the so-called 'active' suspension system, a means whereby a computer controlled the suspension movement. Basically, a car with active suspension went faster than one without. And the Jordan did not have active suspension. I was soon overtaken by Schumacher and a few others. Apart from that, I was really struggling physically. The car was far too small for me and I found that I was really cramped in the cockpit. I knew my back was going to give in before long. I was getting to the stage where the pain was such that I would be unable to continue.

Then it rained! The slower pace, and the fact that the G-forces and the steering load were reduced, meant much of the effort was taken out of driving. Now I could concentrate on stopping for rain tyres. When I asked to come in to the pits, I was told to stay out because my team-mate, Rubens Barrichello, was about to stop. The team wanted to bring him in first, even though he was running behind me on the road. Due to some confusion, however, it was decided that I could come in after all. Unfortunately, they told me on the radio just as I was passing the entrance to the pit lane. That meant a long and comparatively slow lap with slick tyres – in the pouring rain. That lap cost me about 25 seconds.

I eventually made my stop for wet tyres, the next problem being choosing the right moment to go back to slicks once the rain had stopped. Experience had taught me a lot about Suzuka in the rain and I knew I could stay out a bit longer on wet tyres. Hill had changed back to slicks quite early and it was during this period that I had the Ayrton Senna incident, which I described in detail in the opening chapter.

When I made my second pit stop, I rejoined in seventh place. Towards the end of the race, I was catching Derek Warwick at two seconds a lap. I went to sail past him, and he gave me the biggest and the most unlikely chop I've ever had in my motor racing career. Coming out of the 130R – a very fast left-hand bend taken at about 170 mph – he tried to push me into the wall. I couldn't believe it. I wasn't very happy about that, to say the least. It was not what I would have expected from an experienced Grand Prix driver; this was a very crude manoeuvre of the worst kind.

At the next corner, a very slow chicane, I nudged the back of his car and spun him off the road. When I came past at the end of the next lap, he was standing by the edge of the track, shaking his fist. After the race, he told the British press how hard done by he had been. Poor Derek! Okay, I had hit him and pushed him off the road. But nobody saw what had happened 200 yards before. He could have caused a serious accident whereas I had just spun him out at very slow speed.

Tapping someone from behind is a well-known tactic at that particular corner. It's a Suzuka favourite, but I wouldn't do it to someone simply to make up a place. However, if another driver is going to play dirty, I can play the same game. I've no complaint about that, but what really annoyed me was the way in which Derek had acted the innocent with the press. Anyway, I had finished sixth, scored a Championship point in my first Grand Prix and the Warwick incident was quickly forgotten – particularly in the aftermath of my post-race interview with Ayrton Senna!

I flew to Macau on the day after the Japanese Grand Prix. A man was sitting near me on the plane, reading a newspaper. I caught sight of a headline which said: 'Race Ace hit by Senna'. I suddenly felt really embarrassed. It hadn't occurred to me that the incident would be very big news. Straight after the race, I had been involved a big party. I had scored a point in my first Grand Prix. I was Mr Happy.

We had been joking about the business with Senna but I hadn't given it a thought after that. But, everywhere else, it seemed this was a major event. I was amazed to discover much later that the story had made the front page of many of the British newspapers. I wouldn't have minded but for the fact that they had dug out some awful photographs of me!

I was staying in Macau, in my flat which didn't have a telephone. I was completely oblivious to the fact that the world's press was trying to get hold of me. A week later, I flew down to Australia for the final Grand Prix of the season. I had forgotten all about Suzuka until I got off the plane at Adelaide. There were reporters, photographers and television crews everywhere. One of the air hostesses asked who I was. She wanted to know if I was a boxer. I said it was funny she should put it like that...

The fuss soon died down once the Grand Prix got under way – and particularly after I had only managed nineteenth place during qualifying (due to an engine misfire) and then slid off the road in the race itself.

In the meantime, I had to concentrate on the final round of the Japanese F3000 championship at Suzuka. The irony is that I think I would have won the title if I hadn't competed in the Formula 1 races. I went back to Japan immediately after the Australian Grand Prix. There was no time for testing in between, and I more or less went straight into qualifying for the race. The Formula 3000 series in Japan permitted the use of special qualifying tyres which are at their best for just two laps. If you don't do a good time during those two laps, then too bad. I qualified in sixth place which, at Suzuka, is no good if you want to win the race. The competition is so close that it is necessary to qualify in the top three in order to have any hope of getting onto the podium. I needed to finish third. I finished fourth. It was a great shame for everyone in the Cerumo team. But they wanted me to stay the following year.

I was also talking to Jordan about continuing in Formula 1. EJ had signed an option with me whereby if he wanted me to drive, then I had an obligation of sorts to do so. But I told him that I was going back to Japan unless he offered me a better deal. He improved the terms, but not by much, and then took up the option. I was to be a full-time Grand Prix driver for 1994.

Once again, I had mixed feelings. If I had stayed in Japan, I would have earned between US$1.2 million and US$1.3 million. By choosing Formula 1, I was walking away from a lot of money. I was probably safe enough to retire, so long as I lived what you might call a normal existence. But I couldn't have lived the high life if I retired, so I was also walking away from security in a manner of speaking. At the end of the day, however, I reckoned I could always go back to Japan thanks to having such a good reputation there. What I did not bargain for was the recession which was about to hit Japan. As it turned out, I would have earned a fraction of the anticipated figure after just one year. You just never know what the future holds.

Having said that, I had a pretty shrewd idea what to expect when I reached Hockenheim for the German Grand Prix in the Ferrari. I knew the car would be better than it had been at Silverstone. It had to be! I was quite quick on the first day of practice. My times compared to Michael's had been good in the final, twisting section of the track; I was losing out on the long straights which dominate Hockenheim. As a result, I was disappointed with eighth place on the grid.

My involvement with the technical side was minimal due to the continuing problems with the manufacture of parts having curtailed my testing. I didn't feel I knew which way the team was heading. I hadn't had any input when it came to discussing which way we were going on set-up. However, the race itself was reasonable. I closed up on Michael and, in the absence of any instruction to overtake, I held station behind him. The pit stops came and went without any drama. Then my gearbox failed. Michael struggled to finish fourth. Hardly a great race.

With progress being limited to routine work on the test track, I found I was spending quite a bit of time in a recently-installed gym at Fiorano. This came from a suggestion I had made to Jean Todt. At the start of the season, I had been hanging around for a considerable time, waiting to drive the new car. I told Jean I might as well have been in a gym, so he organised the conversation of a room at

Fiorano. They did a fantastic job. It is a really nice gym in which to work out. I'm not particularly good at motivating myself, but I know it has to be done. It is a matter of being sensible and using common sense.

Fitness was not something I had thought much about while racing in the lower formulae but it came into the reckoning once I started in Formula 1. I had done a little bit of running while in Japan but, at the end of 1993, when I made my Formula 1 debut, I was actually very fit thanks to the massive amount of driving I had been doing. I had been racing F3000 and sports cars, and also testing for Dunlop. It was just test, test, test. I was as fit as a fiddle and really sharp.

Michael is the same: he drives all the time. If he is not testing, then he jumps in a go-kart. Each time he gets into the Formula 1 car, he's on the pace immediately. I felt that way at the end of 1993 and I knew I had to at least maintain that level the following year. I started swimming and going to the gym. Eddie Jordan forced me to do that. He threatened a fine of $1000 for each day I failed to go training. I missed a few – but he didn't find out! It was hard work but the effort was worth it.

Formula 1 is physically demanding, much more than any other form of motor racing thanks to the huge G-forces affecting your neck, body and upper arms. It is difficult for anyone watching from the outside to appreciate just how much effort it takes simply to hold the steering wheel. The car never wants to go straight, and when it comes to a corner, it never wants to turn. The driver is fighting the car the whole way round the circuit. And, in the race, that struggle can go on for an hour and 45 minutes. Your hands and arms get very strong, so much so that I noticed that the muscles in my arms had reduced thanks to the power steering on the Ferrari.

It is very difficult to find the best exercise to strengthen neck muscles. In fact, there is no substitute for driving. I find that if I try to exercise my neck, I tend to hurt it because my neck is quite long, which is not ideal for a racing driver. Driving is the best answer and, at Ferrari, I had unfortunately been getting very little of that in 1996. But it had been much worse for a few months at the start of my first full season in Formula 1 two years before.

The season started very badly and I never really recovered. First of all, I had to attend a hearing concerning the Senna incident. It was pretty obvious what had happened during that race and I couldn't see why I should have to travel from Japan, where I was carrying out an important test, to Paris simply to state the obvious. Just because the governing body, the FIA, had demanded my presence at a meeting of the World Motorsport Council, I had to drop everything and run.

I arrived from Tokyo and went to the hearing dressed in the casual clothes – jeans, baseball boots, sports shirt – which I had been wearing during the flight. I couldn't see why I should get dressed up just to give evidence. Once I was in the room, the officials started to discuss the Japanese Grand Prix and ran a video showing what had happened in the race. I was asking myself: 'What's this got to do with getting thumped by another driver?'

Senna was also present, of course. He was claiming I did various things on the track. I couldn't believe what I was hearing. Quite simply, Senna told lies. He claimed I had forced him off the road three times, which was total nonsense. There was not a shred of evidence; just his word against mine. I remember looking at him and thinking: 'How can you sit there and tell blatant lies?' Over the years we had heard Senna talk about his religious and moral values – and then he came out with this. I was absolutely staggered.

The transcript of our 'interview' in the Jordan office at Suzuka was then discussed. That spoke for itself. Senna was totally the aggressor. I didn't swear once, but he constantly swore at me. In the end, Senna received a two-race ban, suspended for six months. I thought that was more than enough; a fine would have been adequate. That, unfortunately, would not be the last time I would visit the FIA headquarters. Events in the opening race of the 1994 season would lead me back to Paris and a severe punishment for an incident in which, I still say to this day, I was clear of all blame.

The Brazilian Grand Prix was 33 laps old and I was in eighth place. I was being chased by Jos Verstappen in a Benetton and we were about to lap the Ligier of Eric Bernard. Ahead of us, Martin Brundle had suddenly run into trouble in his McLaren. Brundle slowed but, because I was tucked under the rear wing of the Ligier, I was not aware of that. We were doing close to 200 mph when Bernard came off the throttle suddenly at a point long before the usual braking area. I was faced with the choice of going right, and off the circuit, or straight into the back of the Ligier, or jinking to the left. I chose the latter.

Things happen so quickly at those speeds, I didn't have time to see where Verstappen was. He was coming up on my left and he swerved and missed me. He keep his foot on the throttle because he thought I was trying to stop him from overtaking. Like me, he was unaware of the slowing McLaren. But once he was in that situation, he didn't lift off. He put a rear wheel on the dirt and went sideways, into my front wheel, which then launched the Benetton into a series of somersaults, the car going over the top of Brundle's McLaren. Martin got a knock on the head but, otherwise, no one was badly hurt. It was a very spectacular accident.

The race officials looked at a video of the incident. When played frame-by-frame, it looked as though I had all the time in the world before pulling out. But, at 200 mph, it was pure instinct. Swerving was the quickest and most obvious way out of trouble. It was decided that I was to blame, for which I received a ban from the next race in Japan and a $10,000 fine.

Jordan decided to appeal. We thought we had a very good case. We brought all the telemetry which showed that nothing was premeditated. It was explained to the appeal court just how much a car slows down (thanks to the drag created by the wings) at those speeds once the driver lifts his foot off the throttle. Even if I had simply hit the brakes, by the time I had done that, I would have been into the back of the Ligier. But they wouldn't have any of that. My ban was extended from one race to three. It was ridiculous; quite unbelievable.

One of the FIA officials actually drew a comparison with a motorway accident, saying a driver would be prosecuted for dangerous driving if he swerved out of his lane. The only reason you would need to do that on a motorway would be because you were running too close to the car in front. That's dangerous. I agree. But that law does not apply in motor racing and how they failed to appreciate that is beyond me. If Verstappen had lifted off the throttle, everyone would have fanned out and overtaken the McLaren. But the officials didn't see it that way.

No one had ever received a punishment as severe as that, particularly for one manoeuvre carried out under mitigating circumstances. Being banned for three races at the beginning of your career is tantamount to being driven out of the sport. That's how I viewed it. They were trying to halt my career right there and then.

Eddie Jordan was excellent. He stood by me all the way – which was a bit of a surprise because, to be honest, who would want to know a driver who had caused so many problems? In my first race, I had been involved in a fight with Senna; in the second, I crashed after 12 laps; in third race, I was held responsible for a multi-car pile-up. I was banned from my fourth, fifth and sixth races. But, in the seventh, I scored a point. Talk about coming into Formula 1 with a bit of a bang!

That comeback Grand Prix, the Spanish, was very difficult. I had to be extremely careful because I knew my every move would be watched; I had the feeling that the officials were out to get me, that they had born a grudge ever since the Senna business. And, of course, the other drivers knew that. They were aware that I could not afford to become involved in an incident of any kind. They could attack and I would have to be careful in how I responded. If there was a problem then, despite the fact that I might be totally innocent, the officials would come down on me like a ton of bricks.

The other problem was that my absence behind the wheel meant I was desperately short on miles and experience. But at least the sixth place in Spain made up for that. In fact, the rest of the season was reasonable although, at the beginning of September, I went into the back of Johnny Herbert at the first corner of the Italian Grand Prix. I had made a very good start and got up to fourth place. Johnny braked too early and I hit the brakes to try and avoid him. He had more or less stopped and I just tapped the Lotus up the rear and spun him out. There was a bit of tyre smoke and it looked like I had locked up all the brakes in a desperate moment. In fact, only the left-front wheel had locked, but it looked much worse than that. Anyway, it was my fault.

The race was stopped and restarted, and I was put to the back of the grid – which wrecked that race from my point of view. I didn't think there was a rule which said the officials could do that. Once again, I think they overstepped the mark. Worse still, I also received a suspended one race ban. In effect, I was punished twice for one offence. Again, that was unprecedented. It began to become apparent that one official in particular had been behind all of these punishments. It was enough to give anyone a persecution complex.

I began to think about going back to Japan. I went as far as contacting my former team to find out how they were fixed. But I didn't go any further than that. Jordan persuaded me to stay and I had a few good races, particularly in Japan where I finished fifth. Whenever you get a good result, everything is rosy again. In the light of my recent exploits with Ferrari in 1996, I needed that sort of boost at the next race in Hungary.

CHAPTER 14

Engineering Success

The few days I had at home between the German and Hungarian Grands Prix turned out to be a worrying time. My jet-ski broke down. This was serious.

The trouble was largely self-inflicted. I liked flying off the water and sliding up the beach, the only problem being that stones were being fired into the works and causing havoc with the pump and the blades. I fitted a new set of blades and the jet-ski was great for a day. Then it broke down again. I began to wonder whether it was me or the machinery. Everything I touched, from a Ferrari to a jet-ski, seemed to break. It made me doubt the wisdom of flying helicopters!

I had actually passed the final exam for my private pilot's licence a few days before leaving for Hungary. I did it in England with Mike Smith, a fantastic pilot. It was tough enough, the most difficult thing for me being the radio work. I had done all of my flying in Ireland where, apart from the routine calls, there is little need to use the radio. When flying in England, there is more traffic to contend with and the radio is in use for much of the time.

It is something else to think about. You need to get into the routine of saying things in the right order. It comes with experience, of course, but I found it very, very tricky. It is necessary to give your registration. Normally I would say Echo India Charlie Golf Uniform, which is the call sign for the helicopter I fly in Ireland, but I was not using that chopper for the exam. So I had to think about the different registration each time. If, say, I was dealing with an emergency, I would have prefaced the call sign with 'Mayday,

Mayday' and then said 'Robinson R22 helicopter with engine failure, auto rotating into field 3000 feet, position three miles south-east of Banbury, heading 288 degrees, private pilot PPLH,' which is my status, and then, 'one person on board, flying solo.' And, of course, while doing all that I would actually be trying to fly the thing! But the radio call has to be in that precise order.

I was tested on a cross-country run, my first in England, in a helicopter which was new to me. My radio work was not very good but I reached my destination without crashing into anyone or anything and then returned just as safely. That earned me my licence. Now I needed a helicopter of my own.

I had met Mike Wheatley, an agent who deals in helicopters and has a reputation for being straightforward to negotiate with. In other words, I was unlikely to be ripped off! I looked at a few helicopters in England but they were too expensive. We found a six-seater Squirrel in Germany. The price seemed reasonable and I thought about it while on my way to Hungary for the Grand Prix. I needed to do something to keep up my morale as I looked to end my run of retirements.

When I qualified in fourth place, people made a lot of fuss and said I had done a good job. Maybe they were being kind or perhaps they did not see the reality of the situation. The fact was that I was almost 1.4 seconds behind Michael, who had qualified on pole position. The car was just as much a struggle as it had been before and I was on the second row only because the Benettons had not got their act together at the Hungaroring. But, having said that, I could think of no better circuit on which to luck into fourth place.

Overtaking is almost impossible on such a tight circuit. Starting from the second row behind Michael and Damon Hill, I felt I had a chance to do something useful in the race. The only problem was, I would be on the right of the grid, but off the racing line and on the dirty side of the track. And, at the Hungaroring, a track which is not used a great deal, the dirty side is extremely dusty and offers very little grip.

I made quite a good start and tried to move to the left but Jean Alesi was already filling that space. Since I did not want to go down the inside – a move which would probably have sent me sliding straight on at the first corner – I had no option but to back off slightly, and that dropped me to fifth.

Since we were concerned about front tyre wear on this circuit, I took it easy for the first six or seven laps. Then I began to push and I caught Alesi very quickly – only to throw all that work away. I touched a kerb on the inside of a fast downhill section and it was enough to cause a spin and drop me behind Gerhard Berger's Benetton. I gathered myself together, caught Berger but then made what turned out to be a very slow pit stop. That gave me with the task of chasing Berger once more. I was closing on the Benetton when the gearbox overheated and left me with no option but to stop. It was the same problem I had experienced two weeks before in Germany. I was very disappointed, to say the least.

I had been confident of finishing on the podium, a result which would have lifted my spirits at a time when the immediate future did not seem to hold any decent prospects. To put it bluntly, there did not appear to be anything happening from my point of view. There was no hope of any worthwhile testing and, at the time, I could see no reason why matters should improve in the short term.

There was no getting away from the fact that I was 1.4 seconds slower than Michael during qualifying. The car was nowhere near what I wanted. If you can't open the throttle – which I could not do on the exit of the corners because the car wanted to understeer straight on – then there is no chance of doing a decent job. I simply could not attack the corners. End of story.

I was being asked by the media once again if I regretted the decision to leave Jordan and join Ferrari. Despite the problems, I had no doubt that I had made the right move. I might have had a more enjoyable year with Jordan, but they weren't getting anywhere. They were having a half-hearted attempt at doing the things which I felt should have been done two years before. Until some pretty drastic steps were taken, the Jordan team would continue to make very little progress.

At Ferrari, I was in a much better position for the future. Nineteen-ninety-six was turning out to be an extraordinarily difficult year for everyone in the team. I couldn't remember the last time Michael Schumacher had scored just 29 points three-quarters of the way through the season. In the past, he would have achieved that in three races. And as for my meagre nine points...

I was with a few friends from Ireland and we were in no hurry to leave Budapest. It is an exceptionally beautiful city but unfortunately the night life does not amount to much. Mind you, it's not particularly hot in any city on a Sunday night. Even Dublin can be quite still – unless you know exactly where to go. I flew back there on Monday. By late afternoon, I was out on the jet-ski, but the respite would be brief.

A few days later, I was off again, a private jet picking me up in Dublin and calling at Biggin Hill in Kent, where David Coulthard and a few of his mates came on board. We were on a mission for Marlboro which included attending a few parties and discos in Belgium. It was all very nice, except that I came down with a bug of some kind and, once the formalities were over, I had to return home very quickly, leaving David to deal with about 15 Marlboro girls. David is pretty fit. I was sure he could cope.

It was back to business on the track a few days after that with a quick visit to Fiorano to do the collaudo in readiness for the Belgian Grand Prix. Then I drove north, stayed overnight in Stuttgart, went to Hanover and bought the helicopter and then motored on to Amsterdam for a night before going across to Spa-Francorchamps.

I wasn't particularly looking forward to the weekend. I thought Spa was going to be a tough circuit for us but, having said that, I was interested in comparing my time through Eau Rouge, a very quick downhill section which twists left and climbs steeply to the right. Everyone says it is a fantastic corner. I don't know what the fuss is all about but, even so, it would provide an interesting comparison.

On that section of the lap, Michael was just five-hundredths of a second quicker. Everywhere else on the circuit, I was much slower. I was losing a full second on the middle section; in fact, I was pretty atrocious through there. This part of Spa is all about having a car which is well balanced. To achieve that, you need to test. As a result, it was no surprise when Michael was third fastest and I was ninth.

There is only so much you can do on a race weekend. A driver will work with his engineer, changing springs and roll bars, trying different wing angles and generally attempting to make the car work to its maximum on the circuit in question. In the case of the F310, the handling problem went beyond mere springs and bars but, even so, my engineer, Luca Baldisserri and I, did the best we could.

I believe that a driver's relationship with his engineer is one of the most important aspects of the business. If you look at the history of motor racing, it becomes obvious that a strong engineer and a strong driver work very well whereas, if you've got a strong driver and a weak engineer, it's not so good. However, a strong engineer and a weak driver could turn out to be a very productive combination.

Many people believe that the engineer sets up the car. He does that initially, but then it's the driver's job to tell him what he wants and the engineer then has to work that into the set-up. The driver and engineer must have a very good understanding. For instance, I can't tolerate mid-corner understeer; I can't live with it and, unfortunately, that has been the problem with the Ferrari. It used to have oversteer when turning in, then mid-corner understeer. Now it just has the understeer. But I can't cope with it.

Because I stayed with the Cerumo team for three years in Japan, they came to understand that. They learned to set the car up so that there was no understeer. As soon as I had it, I lost a lot of time. It was the same with the Jordan. At the end of 1995, everyone was beginning to realise that if I had understeer in a race, I would be off the pace. I did a race distance with Ferrari at Mugello and, during the one stint when we dialled out the understeer, I went half a second quicker every lap.

You need to have a good understanding of the car, which only comes from testing at different places and building up a relationship with the car so that the engineer can appreciate exactly what you want. You get to know what the car is doing, the engineer gets to understand the car and the driver, but all of that only comes from miles at the wheel and a period of time working together. You need to get the basics right in the first place. And, as I said, the engineer needs to be strong.

Of course, I have had a language problem at Ferrari. Luca Baldisserri's English is not brilliant and I don't think he has been helped by my Ulster accent! We have struggled from time to time and things have happened slower than perhaps they should have done as a result. Over a period of time, a driver and his engineer will reach the stage where they need to say very little; there will almost be a kind of telepathic understanding.

You might find it hard to believe, but the best working relationship I have ever had was with Sato San, my engineer for three years at Cerumo in Japan. No-one comes close. He spoke no English and, obviously, I could not speak his language. We communicated through an interpreter. But we spent three years working together. We tested twice a week. I didn't know him any better at the end of it, but he certainly knew me.

He could almost read my mind. He had a natural ability with the car and our relationship began to gell halfway through our second year. By the third season together, we were really close. He was fantastic. Stunning. And, because of the language barrier, I think this proved that psychology does not come into the equation. Some people believe that the engineer is also responsible for motivating the driver and talking him into a competitive state. As far as I am concerned, the engineer simply needs to get the car right and I will do the rest. Sadly, we were struggling during the Belgian Grand Prix.

This was probably the worst race of the season from my point of view. Not only was I slow in qualifying, I was ridiculously slow in the race itself. My best lap was three seconds away from the fastest lap of the race. I think that was the furthest I've been off the pace in my entire motor racing career. It was very frustrating.

Each time I tried to push hard, the car would understeer all the way from mid-corner to the exit. I had felt for some time that there was something not quite right with the steering and this prompted me to mention the problem again. An investigation afterwards at least gave me the minor consolation of discovering that there might be a shortcoming in that area although a quick fix would be difficult to achieve before the end of the season.

The first part of the race wasn't too bad. I made a good start and then got knocked back a couple of places to ninth after being clobbered by a Jordan at the first corner. Martin Brundle had pulled away from me at the start but I began to edge closer to him again. I had just stopped for my first set of tyres, when the Safety Car appeared because of an accident on one of the quick sections at the far end of the track.

The purpose of the Safety Car is to allow the marshals to sort out the mess and clear away any wreckage without being in danger from cars passing at speed. We are supposed to form in an orderly queue behind the Safety Car and tool around until the track is clear. It is a fairly straightforward process although, because the Spa-Francorchamps track, at 4.3 miles, is quite long, it took a while for everyone to form the queue.

I think that's where I made a mistake by not going quickly enough while trying to catch the end of the queue. Yellow warning flags are shown all round the circuit to indicate that the Safety Car is out and the rules say that you should proceed with caution under a yellow. The reason of course is that a yellow, under any other circumstance, only appears at the scene of the incident and it makes sense for drivers to go carefully at that point. But, on these occasions, there is a grey area in the rules when the yellows appear all round the circuit even though the track is clear for 97 per cent of the lap. I don't know whether you are allowed to go flat out to catch up. The yellow flags mean 'slow down' but it is in your interest to go flat out. I believe I should have gone faster than I did. By the time I had latched onto the queue, quite a few of the drivers had taken the opportunity to dive into the pits for fuel and tyres. I'm sure I lost one or two places there.

Michael, on the other hand, had been due to come in at the end of the lap in which the Safety Car first appeared. That was the perfect time to make his stop because he could then rejoin and be at the head of the queue once the others had come in at the end of the next lap. That contributed greatly to his second win of the season.

I noticed that the front end of the car was hitting the track more than it should. At first I thought this was due to the tyre pressures being too low because there was insufficient temperature being generated in the tyres as we crawled along behind the Safety Car.

But, once the race resumed and I pushed really hard in order to increase the temperatures and, hence, the pressures, I found that the trouble with the front end was continuing. I tried to radio the pits to ask for an increase in the pressures on the third set, but they couldn't understand me. Sure enough, the problem continued once I had made my second stop.

Apart from that, I was just plain slow. I couldn't get into the corners quickly because the back of the car was nervous and, as soon as the rear of the car settled, I had understeer when I opened the throttle. Then I found that I was being left behind by a Minardi, one of the back-markers! It was embarrassing beyond belief. Gearbox trouble put me out of misery with fifteen laps to go. What can you say? The answer is very little on a day when Michael pulls off a brilliant win.

The next question was: if Michael could cope, then why the hell couldn't I? I was paying the price for being team-mate with the best driver in the business. It is difficult for observers on the outside to fully appreciate what is going on inside a racing car; if the times are slow, is it the car, or is it the driver? The stopwatch becomes the only arbiter of fact on these occasions and the easiest thing to do is to compare the times of the drivers. It doesn't matter if they are at the front of the grid or at the back; it's the comparison that counts. A is slower than B: end of story. Michael could cope with the terrain and I could not.

Why? The answer was that he had adapted his style to suit. When driving the Benetton, he used to arrive at the corners and turn in early and fast. That's what I like to do. But, watching him in 1996, I could see he was turning in quite late, which is the way you have to drive the Ferrari in order to have a straight exit. I couldn't do that because – and I know this is beginning to become repetitive – I hadn't had the chance to experiment during testing. The simple fact is that you can't turn up on a race weekend and change your technique overnight. I simply did not have the confidence in the car.

There was no point in saying anything because the team understood the problem. They agreed that I was in awful situation and there was no alternative but to bide my time and wait. Everyone was very understanding but it did not remove the frustration. But at least I had a drive with one of the best teams in the business. Damon Hill, the leader of the championship, would not be so fortunate, as he would learn to his cost between Spa and the next Grand Prix in Italy.

CHAPTER 15

Tyre Bashing at Monza

When we arrived at Monza for the Italian Grand Prix, it seemed that no one was interested in the actual racing. The place was buzzing with the news that Frank Williams had kicked out Damon Hill in preference for Heinz-Harald Frentzen as partner to Jacques Villeneuve for the 1997 season. It was a big story, but no one seemed to have the full facts. I wanted to know if Damon had refused Frank's offer. Or was it that Frank simply preferred to have Heinz-Harald?

Whatever the reason, I had a feeling that part of the problem might have been Damon's insistence on having someone conduct the negotiations on his behalf. I have always felt that a driver needs to sit down and talk, one-to-one, with the team owner when important deals are being cut. He needs to be able to read the person he is in discussion with. My manager, Rod Vickery, is very good at what he does but I sat down with Jean Todt and conducted the Ferrari deal myself. It's too important a matter to leave to someone else. It is vital to maintain a good relationship with the team owner and Damon should have been doing everything possible to stay with Williams. Money should have been a considerable way down his list of priorities; the emphasis should have been on talking openly with Frank Williams.

One of the rumours suggested that Damon, through his advisor, had been asking for more money. Whether or not that was the case, I don't know. But I certainly would not want to play a game of poker with Frank. He has always liked to prove that it is his car, rather than the driver, which does the winning and I have to say that he seems to have a point. Look at the hard facts. Frank got David Coulthard into his car in 1995 and David won races. Frank removed Coulthard at the end of the year, and David stopped winning races. I think Damon will find it similar in 1997 and it's a point which Jacques Villeneuve ought to bear in mind. Jacques's management team is quite pushy but, when you drive for Williams, you have to make sure you don't get too big for your boots – otherwise your boots won't be sitting in a Williams for very long. I read in *The Sun* newspaper, just before the British Grand Prix, that Hill was asking Frank Williams for £10 million. I'm sure that the journalist involved, Stan Piecha, would not have written that without inside knowledge. It was immediately obvious to me that Damon would have to start looking for a new job. You don't do that sort of thing with Frank Williams and Hill should have known that.

The point is that Damon Hill is not Michael Schumacher. Agreed, Damon has an excellent strike ratio with 21 wins in just over 60 starts but those statistics mean very little in a Williams. Schumacher delivers in whatever he drives. In my opinion, Hill has not got the same pedigree and so cannot demand the same money, or anything remotely like it.

If Frank offered Damon, let's say for the sake of argument, $7 million – plus, of course, the chance of five or six wins in a season – then what more could Hill want? How much money does he need? As I say, I don't know the full story but, whatever it was, any driver looking for a Williams seat should understand the way it works. And then he should do the talking himself rather than leave it to someone who thinks the smart thing is to go in, make demands and talk big numbers. When it came to 1997 contracts, Frank Williams held all the cards. And that's all there was to it.

Heinz-Harald Frentzen was lucky in so far as Williams gave him a second chance. Frank had asked Frentzen to join the team after Senna had been killed in May 1994. Heinz-Harald had declined the offer, saying he felt he could not walk out on Sauber at a time when their other driver, Karl Wendlinger, had been injured. I told Heinz-Harald he was crazy. You have to grab your chance – and now it had come round for a second time! How lucky can you get?

Nevertheless, I felt Heinz-Harald deserved the seat as much as anyone else in the paddock. He has age on his side and he had made a good job of his drive with Sauber; certainly a better job than he had done before arriving in Formula 1. Anyway, I was pleased for him because he was one of the 'Japanese set' from three or four years before. He is a genuinely nice guy.

While the period between Spa and Monza had been a pretty dramatic time for Hill and Frentzen, things had also been fast-moving for me, but without the sensational effects. Knowing that getting away from Spa can be horrendous due to the traffic, I had arranged for my friend Tony Walsh to take my car to the motorway where I would meet him. The only consolation to be had from an early retirement from the race was an early getaway from the circuit on a motorbike. I met Tony as arranged and we shot off towards the French coast. Not long after the race had finished, Jean Todt called me on the phone. He asked where I was and when I told him that I was in Calais, he just could not believe it! I caught a Shuttle through the Channel Tunnel and reached London in time for an evening out, all of which made that particular Sunday more bearable after the disappointment of the race.

I had no plans to return to Ireland since I was due in Monza for a test the following day. Rather than take a scheduled flight, however, I decided to hire a private jet. We took off from Biggin Hill in Kent and I sat alongside the pilot, flew the plane for a while and practised my radio work. It was a great experience, the only problem being that travelling in such style puts ideas in your head. I quickly decided that nine championship points did not justify the purchase of an executive jet! However, with a rare chance to go testing, there was the thought that I might be able to increase my championship score.

In fact, rain during each day of the Monza test curtailed any useful practice. I was able to try the car without power steering and the fact that I could manage a bit better without it reinforced my feeling that there was something not quite right with the fundamental design of the front of the car. Apart from that, the work carried out at Monza was fairly routine and I was soon back in the private jet for the journey to Ireland.

I had brought another friend, Tom Hicks, along for the trip. Once again I was sitting up front and Tom was in the back, looking after the catering. I had been in radio contact with Geneva, but I had forgotten to flick the switch back to the intercom. I pushed the button and said: 'Tom, could you bring up the sandwiches and drinks – and next time, wear a shorter skirt and a lower-cut top'. Geneva control came back on the radio and said: 'Sorry! Could you repeat that?' They had no idea who it was. We didn't say another word for a couple of minutes...

We were heading towards Weston, my local airfield on the outskirts of Dublin. Weston is a small place owned by Captain Derby Kennedy, one of the first Aer Lingus pilots and, at 81, a great character who still flies when he gets the chance. My pilot could not believe his ears when, on the approach, he discovered the landing fee was £8. 'Are you sure?' he asked. 'This is a Citation jet.' Yes, they were quite sure. The landing fee would be £8. Normally, private jets can expect to pay anything up to £150 for the privilege of landing.

On our way in, we had been asked to hold back because the Gulfstream G4 belonging to the Irish government was about to land at another airfield nearby. As we watched the G4 fly beneath us it struck me as odd that a country as small as Ireland with a population of five million should have the best executive jet in the world. Not even Michael Schumacher can justify owning a Gulfstream G4!

I have to admit that, once again, I was tempted by the thought of buying a jet. The type I had in mind would cost in excess of $1 million and would not be that expensive to run. The point is that the loss on the resale of the aircraft would not exceed $100,000. By my reckoning, it would cost $300,000 to run a jet which, when taking into consideration the cost of flights on commercial airlines, plus the time-wasting inconvenience, is not an extravagance. Agreed, it would take most people ten years and more to earn that sort of money but, when looked at as a percentage of a racing driver's earnings, then it is a different matter.

The plane would be a work tool but I felt I would have a job convincing myself to make the purchase, particularly as I had just bought a helicopter. Owning one of each is for World Champions only although, having said that, there did not seem much point in having one without the other. It takes an hour to reach the airport by road whereas a helicopter can make the trip in eight minutes.

I decided I would have to do a few more good deals such as the taxi company I had acquired a few months before. I had bought LA Cabs in Bangor and business in and around the seaside town near where I was born had turned out to be surprisingly good. I look upon the taxi company as an outside interest and a source of income when I stop racing. An investment like that made more sense that putting money in the bank and I was very pleased with the results.

I was also adding to the value of my house in Dalkey by building a garage with a gym. The local planning authority had taken a look at the house and they had been very pleased with the work I had already done, particularly the use of old stone and granite on the patio. I had to thank the architect for that. He had made the place really nice; modern, but not flashy on the inside and retaining the essential character on the outside. The garage will be built of granite to match the surrounding properties. Well, most of them, anyway. One or two of the houses which have been built in recent years are monstrosities. Anyone who can afford to buy a plot of land in an expensive suburb such as Dalkey ought to be able to afford to build their house in natural stone. In fact, I feel they ought to be forced to do it that way.

My property used to be the gardener's cottage within the grounds of a large house. It has two floors, although the top level is, in fact, the attic, but it is the perfect size as far as I am concerned. It is easy to maintain and Derek Sloane, an old friend of mine from Northern Ireland, has the job of keeping it tidy and looking after my interests while I am on my travels. The owner of the main house very kindly allows me to use his tennis court and swimming pool, so I have all the benefits without the worry of the upkeep. Derek and I regularly play tennis and, even though he looks overweight, he beats me every time. He is solid muscle and I have never seen anyone accelerate so quickly. Each time I knock the ball into the far corner, with Derek stranded on the opposite side of the court, I think I've won the point because it will be impossible for Derek to reach the ball. But he is like a cartoon character, dust at his feet and a 'whoosh!' as he suddenly appears in the corner and returns the ball. Playing tennis with Derek usually turns out to be pretty bad for my morale. And I wasn't sure if my confidence was about to be lifted by events during the Italian Grand Prix.

I was actually a bit concerned about turning up at Monza and facing the Ferrari fans. I would have felt much happier if I could have honestly said that I had been doing a respectable job on their behalf. The Ferrari supporters were desperate for a good result and I didn't have a hope of giving them one. When they cheered me on, I felt a bit of a fraud. But there was nothing I could do about it.

I was surprised at how quickly I had become known. It was a lovely morning on the day before practice began and I thought I would walk through the park which leads to the track. I was wearing scruffy clothes and I felt sure that no one would expect to come across a Ferrari driver wandering through the park. Some chance! I was spotted by some fans on bicycles – and that was it. While it would be nice to be able to take a walk in peace, it is impossible not to be impressed by their passion for motor racing in general and Ferrari in particular. I noticed a couple walking their dog. The dog had a Ferrari patch on its coat. That's serious!

Everyone asked me how I thought I would get on in the Italian Grand Prix and the trouble was, I didn't know what to say. When I was with Jordan, I always had a reasonable idea about the lap time I could reasonably expect to do and where I might be on the starting grid. Given my experiences with the Ferrari, it was impossible to make a prediction of any kind.

On my first run during qualifying, the car was pivoting too much around the front end. I couldn't turn into a corner with confidence because the car would snap into oversteer. On the exit of the corner, the car felt good but it was hopeless – from my point of view at least – on the way in. At that stage, I was eighth fastest and about half a second down on Berger and Alesi in the Benettons. I thought I might be able to beat them, but that was about it. I would be unable to do anything about the McLarens (which were on form at Monza), and I was a second off Michael's best time.

We adjusted the front wing, but that made the car understeer the minute I opened the throttle on the way out of the corner. Once again, I was finding that the F310 would be good, either on the way in to a corner, or on the way out, but never both at the same time. Nonetheless, I finally managed to do a reasonable lap and qualify seventh despite making a couple of small mistakes. I beat Berger's time and just missed Alesi's by a few hundredths of a second. Better still, I was only four tenths of a second away from Michael in third place, the closest I had been to him for a long time. Despite all of that, I knew this was going to be a tough race.

I really needed a good start on race day, but we had been experiencing clutch problems throughout the weekend. My initial getaway was good but then the clutch suddenly bit and the engine died. To make matters worse, someone had dropped a lot of fluid – I think it was Hill's Williams on pole position – and I half spun the car, losing even more momentum. Fortunately, I had decided to reduce the rear wing angle in the interest of finding more performance on the straight and, even though I was slow initially, I was able to accelerate back up to speed quite quickly. Then all hell broke loose at the first chicane. There were cars going in all directions. Before I knew what was happening, I was in fourth place. I remember thinking: 'This is handy!'

Michael was third and I could see that he wasn't pulling away. I pushed as hard as I could but then he started to extend the gap. Because we had anticipated trouble with my front brakes – it's a problem which affects everyone to a greater or lesser degree at Monza due to the severe braking necessary from high speed into the three chicanes – my brakes had been biased towards the rear. I needed more braking on the front in order to go faster but, if I altered the adjustment, I would have difficulty finishing the race. Fourth place became third when Damon Hill touched a pile of tyres and spun out of the lead. This was looking even better.

Rubens Barrichello was fourth and I was leaving the Jordan behind at around one second a lap. Even if he was making one stop less than me (and therefore running with more fuel on board), Barrichello appeared to be struggling. The next question was:

should I cruise home or should I push hard and keep in touch with Schumacher and Alesi?

I didn't want to cruise. I wanted to get stuck in and catch Alesi, who was now in second place. I would not have felt any satisfaction in easing my way onto the podium. I wanted to race. I wanted to push the leaders all the way. I had more or less written off the year, so I thought I may as well go as hard as I could. If I had backed off, I would have reached the podium and thought: 'Well, I'm only here because everyone else broke down and I was two seconds a lap off the pace'. I didn't want that. So I pushed hard. And then I clipped the tyres which had been piled on the kerbs at the chicanes.

One way or another, the tyres were to cause problems for several drivers. But there was no getting away from the fact that something had to be done, and tyres seemed to be the best answer. The trouble had been caused by the circuit owners placing lower kerbs at the chicanes in order to help the motorbike racers. The previous kerbs were too steep for the bikes but the new ones were too low for the cars. We were going straight over them and, as a result, chunks of concrete were being pulled from the area behind the kerbs and pitched onto the track.

They placed a pile of tyres at each trouble spot but I felt that just one tyre would have been enough since it would have slowed us down if we hit it and yet it would not have caused a broken suspension. At worst, the single tyre would have thrown the car into the air briefly but it would also have prevented drivers from gaining an advantage by cutting across the kerbs. A pile of tyres would certainly stop kerb-hopping, but the consequences would be much more severe, as I was to find out.

As I turned in to a left-hander, the rear of the car stepped out of line slightly and that had the effect of pulling me closer to the pile of tyres on the inside kerb. I didn't think I was going to hit them and I carried on as normal without attempting to take avoiding action. When I looked at the video afterwards, I could see that were three white tyres and a black tyre which was sitting slightly proud. I hit the black tyre. I hadn't been looking at it. In the normal sequence of events, I would have glanced at the tyres and then focused on the track ahead. The black tyre would not have registered fully but the white ones would. I can only assume that's what happened.

The top wishbone of the left-front suspension had been bent. There was nothing for it but to pull to one side and retire. Of course, now was the time to say that I should have backed off and cruised home. A podium finish at Monza would have been fantastic, particularly after such a long run of retirements. I was absolutely gutted as I walked back to the pits. Nineteen-ninety-six seemed an even bigger disaster than ever. I had become immune to the catalogue of problems over the past few months. But this really hurt.

Michael won the race, which was good and bad from my point of view. It was bad because it rubbed salt in the wound. But it was great for the team and, of course, Monza went absolutely wild over a Ferrari victory. Michael had also touched the same pile of tyres. In fact, he hit them so hard that the steering wheel had been wrenched from his right hand. But he had got away with it. So nothing was said about my mistake.

I knew I was not concentrating enough when driving. Even during practice, I found that I could not focus for a full lap. It may seem a strange thing to say when sitting behind the wheel of a 200 mph car with 700 bhp under your right foot, but my mind was all over the place. It's like any job; if you don't do it enough, then you lose your sharpness. The Formula 1 cars accelerate so fast that if you are a little bit late on the throttle, then it adds up during the course of a lap. It's the same if you brake that little bit early. You can do all the gym work you want, but your brain is not being trained to drive a car. I need to drive for a minimum of two days each week in order to keep my mind focused. Throughout the summer, all I had to occupy me was jet-skiing, tennis and unimportant things.

Having said that, I went to Estoril and carried out some tests with the engine which we planned to use in 1997. The new V10 felt very good. It was more driveable than the current engine and it had a bit more power. But the most important thing was to make an early start for the 1997 season. And, apart from getting more miles behind the wheel, it was a good feeling to have some input into next year's car. Monza was already a distant memory.

CHAPTER 16

What is Damon Really Like?

The test at Estoril confirmed my thoughts about the lack of time spent behind the wheel of the F310 and its detrimental effect on my driving. When official practice for the Portuguese Grand Prix at Estoril got under way, I found my concentration was better and I was more focused. It had happened after each test in the past. I think a driver can afford to miss one or two sessions, but a gap of three or four months has a serious effect. If you had suggested that at the end of 1995, I would have said that it was rubbish, just an excuse. But Estoril confirmed the growing doubts I had experienced throughout the season. Having said that, I then went and made a small but costly error during qualifying!

The car was more or less as before but the lower temperatures seemed to stabilise the rear of the F310; generally, it felt quite good. My first two runs were quicker than Michael's. On my third run, I made a mistake going into a very tight left-hander at the back of the circuit, a really ridiculous corner which interrupts the flow of an otherwise challenging circuit. I braked in the usual place but, in my enthusiasm to go even faster, I just braked that little bit harder and locked the wheels. I had to come off the pedal and back on again in order to release the brakes. The fraction of a second it took to do that meant I ran past the apex of the corner and lost about 0.25 seconds. That cost me fourth place on the grid – perhaps third – and to make matters worse, Michael improved his time which meant he was fourth and I was sixth. We were separated by 0.13 seconds, which was quite reasonable. Even so, I was annoyed with myself because I felt I could have been quicker than Michael for the first time since the opening race of the season in Melbourne.

You can never underestimate the psychological damage which is done by a run of bad results. Finishing at all costs becomes a top priority and that affects your thinking, as I found when the field rushed into the first corner. I had made a good start and got ahead of Berger, but I was just too cautious and Gerhard sailed around the outside of me at the first corner. As the race began to settle down, I kept pushing to keep in touch with the Benetton. There was nothing between us. It was stalemate until a good pit stop by the Ferrari mechanics allowed me to take sixth place and pull away quite easily from Gerhard.

Everything was fine until my final stop, when I fitted a brand new set of tyres. These had not been scrubbed during practice. The process of scrubbing, which takes just a few laps, puts the new rubber through a heat cycle which then leaves the tyres in better shape for the race. The heat cycle raises the temperature quite dramatically but, once the tyres have cooled and are then run again in the race, the temperature is not as high and the rubber is more consistent. In effect, the temperatures on this set of tyres were too high, which meant the pressures were up and that had a bad affect on the handling of the car.

I was really struggling and Gerhard began to reel me in. But I knew it would be difficult for him to overtake unless I either made a mistake or had a problem with a backmarker. That moment came with a few laps to go when I caught a Minardi on the approach to a corner. I pulled out to overtake and then made sure I braked as late as I possibly could. I knew that would not allow me to get around the corner in text-book style but, the point was, I was aware that Gerhard was coming down the inside, on my left, and he would wait until I braked before he hit the middle pedal.

I waited until the last possible moment before slamming on the brakes. Gerhard sailed up the inside – and straight on. He was going much too fast to make the corner. I had the advantage in that I brake with my left foot, which means I can do it quicker than Gerhard, who uses his right foot in the more traditional manner which requires a fraction of a second to move from one pedal to the other. I had done the same thing to Berger during the Belgian Grand Prix. He had spun on that occasion and here he was in trouble again! I think he's still trying to work it out...

The net result was that I was able to nip past him again. I felt fairly comfortable. I was cruising round, taking the corners as cleanly as I could and generally making sure I left Gerhard with no opportunity to overtake. However, knowing Gerhard, I was sure he would try something on the last lap. As we went into the tight hairpin at the back of the circuit, I ran down the inside, just to make sure he had no room to have a go. Then, Boof! The Benetton rammed the back of my car and spun me round. Luckily, I had managed to engage the clutch and keep the engine running. I was able to turn the car around and carry on. Berger, meanwhile, was off the road, his front suspension broken. You would think that would have been the end of him. Not Gerhard!

Sadly, the television cameras failed to catch any of this. It was the most incredible sight as Berger came flying out of the gravel trap, stones flying everywhere, his suspension up in the air with me trying to get past him. There had been no other battles worth watching by this stage – Villeneuve had won the race from Hill to keep the Championship open until the last race in Japan – but here was a crippled Benetton and a damaged Ferrari tripping over each other as they tried to reach the finishing line. I was amazed and disappointed to discover that the cameras had missed it. If nothing else, this underlined the point that Grand Prix racing needs a permanent director who can read the race and make sure the job is done properly. Otherwise, a lot of the action is missed and the races seem boring. This was a classic example.

As we came through the last corner, I was determined to get my fifth place back again. But I knew Gerhard, who was really struggling now, would take me with him if he could. It would have been similar to Schumacher taking Hill out of the final race and the 1994 Championship in Adelaide, or Prost and Senna at Suzuka in 1989. 'Oops, sorry! Didn't see you there...' That sort of thing. I had to make sure Gerhard would have no excuse. If he was going to take me off, it would have to be blatantly obvious. I waited until there was a short straight and then moved as far away from the Benetton as possible and nipped through.

I took the chequered flag in fifth place: two points at last. It was nice to make it to the finish and beat Berger in the process because Ferrari and Benetton were having a close battle in the Constructors' Championship, Michael having held off Alesi to take third place, the combination of these two results placing Ferrari just one point ahead of Benetton with one race to go.

We had an unusual situation after the race in that most of the drivers were staying in Estoril for a test the following week. Instead of rushing to catch helicopters and planes, most drivers and team members went to Coconuts, a night club and disco in the nearby seaside resort of Cascais. Michael may not have been going home but he was flying nonetheless. I don't know what he had been drinking but it put him into the sort of frisky mood where he likes to throw water over everyone. It was an excellent evening and it made a change to able to socialise with racing people.

I never get to see the other drivers away from the race track and, even if I did, there are not that many I would want to spend an evening with. I like David Coulthard a lot; he's a really good bloke. There is very little malice in him and he seems to be a fairly rounded character. I used to meet Frentzen and Villeneuve when we were in Japan. Jacques likes to enjoy himself and Heinz-Harald is a really nice guy. Damon Hill can be very witty and good company but, even though we live quite close in Ireland, our life styles are very different and our paths never cross.

I never know what to make of Damon, particularly as a driver. Looking at the hard facts, Villeneuve arrived at Williams in 1996 and he gave Damon a very difficult time, particularly towards the end of the season. It was the same with Coulthard in the latter half of 1995; he got the upper hand eventually and Damon did not look good by comparison.

Villeneuve's performance at Estoril was a typical example. Jacques made a bad start but then he was very clinical about the method of his recovery and his eventual victory. I have the impression that, if Damon had been in a similar situation, he would not have made such a good job of the recovery and perhaps been a bit more hesitant when coming through the field. It would not surprise me if that was one of the reasons why Frank chose to part company with Damon. It could be that Frank Williams simply felt Damon is not the man to beat Schumacher. I have to say I would agree with that. Then again, nobody in equal equipment could beat Schumacher. There are a couple of drivers who could take him on in slightly superior cars but, even then, I don't think Damon is the man.

My views on Damon are also affected by the memories I have of racing against Jacques. I never thought Jacques was outstandingly quick. Aggressive, very clever and as hard as nails, yes. But not supremely quick. He has done the job I thought he would do at Williams. His move on Michael at Estoril was very impressive. It was not on, of course, unless they were held up by a back-marker but, when the moment came, Jacques seized his chance. Most drivers wouldn't have gone for it. Jacques placed himself in Michael's hands to a certain degree and I know a few drivers who would have run a bit wide and forced Jacques onto the dirt. Michael played very fair and made room for him. It was a great manoeuvre. Most of us would not have thought of attempting a move like that because, in Formula 1, we do not go round the outside of that corner. There is no doubt that Jacques's experience and mentality honed by Indycar racing on ovals came into play there.

I will be interested to see how he compares with Frentzen in 1997. Heinz-Harald was my team-mate for a while in Europe and I know he is very quick. I think his main problem is dealing with pressure. If the 1997 Williams is really good and Frentzen proves quicker than Villeneuve, then Heinz-Harald will walk it. If not, I think he will have a lot of shunts and incidents. He has great car control, but, as some of his performances in 1996 have proved, pressure is not his friend. Whenever he was with me in Formula 3000, I was usually quicker than him and he would be spearing off the road all the time in an attempt to keep pace. He seemed unable to find his limit. He would push and push and, then, bang! Off he would go. Nonetheless, I'm glad he got the Williams drive because I believe he has more natural talent than Damon. But it remains to be seen whether or not he will do as good a job as Damon has done overall. This is Heinz-Harald's big chance; the rest is up to him.

I might have created the impression earlier that Jean Alesi is a hopeless case based on one or two incidents during the season. In fact, I think he has done a very good job. He has been very solid; and has finished most of the races. I don't understand why he insists on criticising his team at all times; it just doesn't make sense. He obviously becomes hot-headed and starts saying things that he probably regrets later on, but, as an Italian speaker and a former driver with Ferrari he ought to know that the Italian journalists will pick up on everything he says and print it. With the British press, or most of them anyway, I can say certain things and know I won't read about it the next day. The Italian press are under much more pressure to produce than the British journalists and Alesi seems to get himself into trouble that way. However, there's no getting away from the fact that he is a very good driver, despite such a bad start to the season.

I can't be so definite about Mika Hakkinen. He certainly looks quick. You see him go over the kerbs and onto the grass; he's all over the place. Then Coulthard will arrive, in totally unspectacular fashion, and do a faster lap. So there appears to be something missing in Mika's repertoire. Ron Dennis, the McLaren boss, is a great supporter of Mika. He really stood by him, particularly after a bad accident at the end of the 1995 season. I think Ron remembers the day that Mika out-qualified Senna. That was just one performance but it seems to sustain Ron. At the end of the day, however, Hakkinen is a quick driver and there aren't many of those around. But in my opinion the complete package is lacking.

Gerhard Berger, despite being one of the oldest drivers, is still fast when the moment is right. He is very good at making things happen for him within the team but he is no longer a top-class runner. He's not going to win a Grand Prix that he doesn't deserve to win whereas you always felt that Prost or Senna or, nowadays, Schumacher might pull something from the bag.

We are talking in comparative terms here because all of the Formula 1 drivers are fast. Michael has the edge over everyone although, if any of the other top drivers can get their cars absolutely right, then there will be nothing in it. But if Schumacher makes his car better than anyone else then he won't be beaten, no matter what the opposition may do. It was exactly the same with Ayrton Senna; if he had his car working well then the rest may as well have stayed at home.

I remember following Senna's progress in the junior Formulae in the early eighties. I was not aware of a special aura or anything like that but he won everything on his way to Formula 1. His death at Imola was such a shock and a terrible shame, especially for his native Brazil where he was *the* national hero. You just had to look at the actions of the Brazilian football team when they won the World Cup in 1994 and paraded an enormous flag emblazoned with the words 'Senna Lives'. The point was, Ayrton Senna got through to people who didn't know about motor racing and didn't care about it. But they cared he was winning – for Brazil. He helped lift the Brazilian people from the terrible conditions most of them live under. Senna was like a God to them.

I can't discuss heroes without mentioning John Watson, the Belfast youngster who was taking on the world at the time and winning Grands Prix. I followed his progress with great interest. When I met 'Wattie' for the first time, I was overawed at first but, as I got to know him, I became increasingly surprised that this was the man who had won five Grands Prix, some of them in very impressive style. I couldn't imagine how such a diffident character could manage a thing like that! John is a decent man who means well, but I was disappointed when he chose not to support me in court at the time of the Brazilian Grand Prix hearing in 1994. I needed a respected driver with John's experience to explain about the performance of Formula 1 cars, and how a driver might react when faced with such a split-second decision. John said he couldn't do it. I was disappointed; I thought he had more backbone than that.

As I said before, Eddie Jordan and the team gave me tremendous support during such a difficult time. That means a lot to a driver in a business where pressures can come from all directions. For that reason, I appreciate my good relationship with Jean Todt. I am honest with him and I think he has been totally honest with me. A few times this year I have given him a hard time but I felt I had to start making it known that I was not particularly happy. It registered with Jean and he came back with arguments which, I have to say, were justified. But I felt I had to make my point.

The only problem is that Jean tends to mollycoddle me a bit too much! I prefer to manage on my own but, like most people, Jean thinks that if I am left to my own devices, I will miss the boat, or whatever. I seem to have that reputation! In fact, I enjoy 'doing my own thing'. I will bring a mate along when I travel so that we can have a good laugh. But, otherwise, I prefer not to travel with an entourage. For instance, I don't feel the need, like some drivers, to have my manager or my family in close attendance wherever I go. I like to have total independence without worrying about what everyone else may be doing.

Sonia, my sister, is the only person who is never far away at the race meetings. She is a qualified physiotherapist but she also looks after my diet and other details. She is very efficient, and so good at what she does. At present, Sonia has her own private practice in Kent but, in 1997, she will be working for me full time in Ireland, looking after property deals and any other business arrangements I may have, in between carrying out general physiotherapy on me. We're close, but in true brother and sister fashion, we don't go out together and we don't spend hours on the phone. It's one of those relationships where very little needs to be said. Sonia started working with me this year at the races and it has been very successful. She is absolutely fantastic. Apart from looking after the food and the physiotherapy, Sonia does a lot of the general routine business such as sorting out passes and arranging other matters. I know I can let her get on with it in the knowledge that the job will be done. I can trust Sonia one hundred per cent and that's a great feeling because it allows me to concentrate fully on the job of driving and integrating with the team.

Before I went to Ferrari, there were some people who believed that the management would have trouble with me and my attitude. In fact, the only thing which Jean Todt has spoken to me about is my dealings with the press. He keeps telling me I have to be very careful.

I understand that but it seems to me that I can't win. For instance, I was stuck in Milan one day and I decided to go to Monza and watch the testing even though I would not be driving. I was talking to some members of the Jordan team when an Italian journalist walked over and asked if I was going back to Jordan. I said no, and asked him why he should think that. When he said it was because I was in the Jordan garage, I explained that I was chatting with my friends and I was watching the testing.

The next day, his newspaper carried a story which said I was leaving Ferrari to go to Jordan. Worse still, the newspaper quoted me as saying that I had no chance at Ferrari while Schumacher was there. Naturally, Jean Todt wanted to know what this was all about. I said it was pure make-believe. How could I be careful under circumstances like that? If the journalist makes it up, what is the point in worrying? So long as everyone in the team knows the story is rubbish, then it doesn't matter.

Before leaving for the final race in Japan, I stopped off at John Barnard's office in England, just to keep up to date with future plans. I found I was dealing with John more and more as the year went on. He is very straightforward, very rational. John has been one of the first to appreciate the difficulties with the car although, in fairness, I have to say that he stuck to the spirit of the rules rather than the letter when it came to the cockpit design. As I said earlier, I think the manner in which this was handled by Williams and Jordan was wrong. I continue to believe that they should have been forced to change their cars at the start of the year. Their interpretation of the cockpit design was within the rules of the sport, but not as those rules were meant to be taken.

Anyway, that was irrelevant as far as John and I were concerned as we went through his plans for 1997. I enjoy discussions of that nature because I am amenable to suggestions and I have a very open mind. I came away very excited about the 1997 car. In fact, life in general was pretty good because I was on my way to Japan and Suzuka, a country and circuit I enjoy. The 1996 season may have been about to close but I felt there was one last chance for me.

173

CHAPTER 17

End of Term in Tokyo

It's surprising how little things can catch you out. I arrived in Tokyo ten days before the Japanese Grand Prix in order to have some time to visit my old haunts. Adam Cooper, the British journalist who had covered Formula 3000 in Japan during the time I had been racing there, travelled with me and one of our first stops after arriving was the President Hotel.

We were both surprised and pleased to find the famous bicycle, which everyone had used as a means of transport, parked in its usual place. But we were taken aback when we realised that Jeff Krosnoff had been the last to use it. He had put his helmet sticker on the frame; the bike, covered in dust, was exactly where he had left it.

It was a very poignant moment for us both. We were there to enjoy ourselves but that sort of flashback just stops you in your tracks. I immediately thought of how Jeff and I had planned that one day we would get everyone back to Tokyo and have a big party. Now, with Jeff and 'Ratzi' both gone, that was not going to happen.

Adam and I went to the clubs and places we knew from the past and, throughout, Jeff's name kept cropping up. 'We did this with Jeff here'… 'Do you remember the time Jeff did that?' And so on. Even though Jeff didn't drink, he was always in our company, having a good time. Had the accident not happened, I'm sure he would have flown specially to Tokyo to join in the fun and tell us all about his Indycar programme.

We went to the clubs he would have known, places such as the Lexington Queen where the owner, Shiga, sent over bottles of champagne. We went to the Hard Rock Café and to Motown, a very small club where they play really good music. Motown becomes very crowded during the weekend, which is why we chose to go on the Monday night when it was almost empty and we could enjoy the music of Van Morrison and the Rolling Stones until the small hours of the morning. Along the way, I met a few people from Cerumo, the Formula 3000 team I raced with in Japan. We had a ball. It was difficult to tear myself away and travel the 300 miles west to Suzuka for the final race. After the first few laps of practice, I almost wished I had stayed in Tokyo.

I could tell straight away that the car was not going to work very well at Suzuka. On paper, it looked good as Michael and I set the fastest times during the first session – but that was only because the track was wet. I knew we would be in trouble once the rain stopped and, sure enough, I was miles off the pace once we put on slick tyres and picked up speed.

Suzuka is the third-longest track on the calendar. It has a very good mixture of corners – apart from the very tight chicane at the end of the lap, which is just plain stupid – and the essential thing is to have a car which, above all else, is nicely balanced. The McLaren, for example, may not have been super-efficient, but it was very well balanced going through the corners. The Ferrari was not. Each time I braked, the car would slide into oversteer and, as soon as I started to power out of the corner, the car began to understeer. I knew it was going to be a struggle.

Having said that, qualifying went much better than I thought it would. Michael was third fastest and I was sixth, just under one second behind. I actually thought I might have been fifth, or perhaps fourth, but my engine, for some strange reason, was slower than Michael's through the speed trap even though we were running an identical amount of wing angle; in other words, I was not carrying more wing in search of downforce in the corners and then paying the price by creating drag on the straight. The engine was not as powerful, and that's all there was to it.

I also had a problem with my final set of tyres not being heated and then, into the bargain, Gerhard Berger deliberately held me up on my last lap. I would be hearing more from Berger before the weekend was finished.

Suzuka lived up to its reputation as a madhouse when it comes to being mobbed by the race fans. They are nuts about Grand Prix racing and that makes life very difficult. The circuit hotel may be only ten minutes walk from the paddock gate but the drivers have to make the journey by scooter or car. Some even use a helicopter. It's quite a problem because, if you stop to sign one autograph, then you are immediately engulfed and rooted to the spot. The Japanese, although very polite, can be extremely persistent.

Suzuka has been noted for massive crowds. Formula 1 was been so popular in the past that ticket holders were decided by lottery but I noticed a fall in the numbers this year. Soccer has really taken a hold in Japan and Grand Prix racing lost a lot of its appeal following Ayrton Senna's death in 1994. He was a hero in Japan, almost as much as he was in Brazil. I don't know if that was because Senna won all three of his championships at Suzuka but, certainly, the drop in Japan attendances has been yet another consequence of his accident at Imola.

Naturally, the publicity attached to the loss of such a well-known name in 1994 focused attention on motor racing and produced comment, a lot of which was uninformed. I think there was a bit of over-reaction by the FIA because something had to be seen to be done, whether it was the right thing or not. The pressure to react in some way or other was too great to allow the governing body to take the sensible course and let everything calm down before taking a careful look at what needed to be done.

In general terms, I think there was an over-reaction on the work done to the circuits, and an under-reaction concerning the changes made to the cars. Reducing the engine capacity from 3.5 to 3 litres was not enough. They should have cut the engine size to 2.5 litres. In fact, I think it really should have been dropped to 2 litres because that equates to the engines used in road cars. There are very few road cars with 2.5 litre engines and none which are 3 litre.

I think the change to 3-litres was the wrong thing to do. At best, it should have been 3 litres for one year, and 2 litres the next. The problem is that the cars are just too damn quick these days. They are quicker with 3-litre engines than they were with 3.5 litres. I don't know how the sport's governing body can justify making changes one year and none the next. The designers are so clever and the technology so advanced that they can regain any performance loss almost straight away.

It has been suggested that one answer would be to reduce the amount of downforce in order to slow the cars in the corners and increase the braking distances by making the braking less effective. But that does not get away from the problem of having too much power. By reducing downforce, the straight-line speed will increase. And, with the power we have, the cars will be like rockets on the straights. It is engine capacity which needs to be tackled. This must be a major step rather than fiddling around with small changes.

On the circuit front, they did a good job with the alterations introduced at Imola. At other places, such as Blanchimont at Spa, I think they over-reacted. Blanchimont is a very fast left-hander taken flat-out at around 170 mph. In my opinion, that corner is worse than before because they took the barrier away from the side of the track and moved it back. If the barrier is at the side of the road, you are going to hit it hard. But it will be a glancing blow, so it's not a problem. It's the same principal they work on with the concrete walls which line the ovals in Indycar racing. The walls look daunting but, in the event of trouble, the car is into the concrete, usually at a shallow angle, straightaway.

At Spa, they have added a sand trap which is a total waste of time. Unless you make the run-off area at least 150 metres long, there's no point in doing anything. The one at Blanchimont is too small. It rises and then, because the wall at the back is not high enough, the sand trap falls away again. The effect is to make a wayward car take off, go straight over the wall and into the trees. It's ridiculous. I asked one of the officials why this had been approved and he more or less said it was a case of doing a bit at a time. He said he didn't want to rock the boat too much!

On the understanding that no circuit can ever be completely safe, Suzuka is reasonable from that point of view. Certainly, it was good place to stage the final shoot-out for the 1996 World Driver's Championship between Jacques Villeneuve and Damon Hill. Villeneuve had to win the race in order to claim the title with Hill finishing outside the top six. But if Damon scored just one point, then the championship would be his. The stage was set when the two Williams drivers qualified on the front row of the grid.

Jacques didn't do his chances any good when he made a terrible start. I passed him on the run down the hill. In fact, my start had been so effective, that I found myself running round the outside of Michael Schumacher as we went through the first corner. I was thinking: 'Jeez, what do I do now?' I knew Michael would be quicker than me over the course of the race, so I dutifully fell in behind him. Initially, Michael pulled away from me but then I started to close the gap; I was actually making up quite a bit of ground each time at the end of the straight.

I knew that Villeneuve, with absolutely nothing to lose, would be on a charge and, sure enough, by lap six the Williams was on my tail. He was much quicker than me but he couldn't overtake. In the end, I felt a bit guilty about holding him up and getting in the way of the championship, so I made it easy for Jacques at the chicane, let him overtake and get on with it. That dropped me to fifth but, even so, at the end of lap 15 Michael and I were only 4.5 seconds apart.

Michael made his first routine stop at the end of the next lap and I came in as I finished lap 18. By the time I rejoined, the situation had changed completely. I was nine seconds behind and Hakkinen's McLaren had overtaken me during the pit stops. My stop had seemed quick enough but a study of the lap times later showed that my entry and exit laps had been slower than Michael's and that had made all the difference.

The second stint was pretty lonely. I managed to stay ahead of Brundle's Jordan and I could just about keep Hakkinen in sight. After my second and final stop, I rejoined behind Brundle. I pulled alongside the Jordan as we came out of the hairpin and he moved over and thumped my right-front wheel, which did the car's handling no good at all. Even so, I eventually managed to get ahead and take fifth place.

That became fourth not long after when, in a dramatic moment which settled the championship, Villeneuve lost a rear wheel and the Williams careered off the track. The wheel bounced across the gravel trap and cleared a spectator fence. I couldn't believe it that no one had been hurt.

With twelve laps to go, my fourth place was under attack from Berger but I was confident because I had set up my car to work well through Spoon Curve, the corner at the far end of the circuit which leads onto the long back straight. I knew from experience that if your car works well through Spoon then nobody as a chance of getting close enough to overtake. Berger, the fastest man on the track at the time, was recovering from an incident earlier in the race. He had tried an overambitious move while attempting to take the lead from Hill. I was to learn at first hand just how stupid he had been as he tried the same thing with me.

I had turned into the chicane and, before I knew what was happening, there was a mighty bang and the Ferrari was launched into the air and it almost rolled over. I don't know what Berger thought he was doing but there was no way he could overtake at that point. That made it two races in a row where he had driven into me. Afterwards, he said 'Sorry'. I told him that once was fair enough. Twice was ridiculous.

Gerhard has had far too many incidents of this type. Almost hitting Hill, a driver who has a chance of the World Championship, is simply unbelievable for someone of Berger's experience. At times like that, you are a bit player when it comes to getting involved with a driver who has a chance of achieving a life time's ambition. Taking the risk of running into the back of a contender and possibly costing him the World Championship is just beyond belief.

I felt Berger deserved to be ripped apart by the press but I didn't think it would happen. Gerhard would get off lightly because everyone would say he is a nice guy; it's amazing how well that works, because he has been around for such a long time. At the end of the day, someone who regularly takes people off the track is not a nice guy. I know I have to be careful here in the light of what I did to Derek Warwick in 1993 at the very same corner but, as I explained in an earlier chapter, there were extenuating circumstances. To the best of my knowledge, I had not attempted to drive Berger off the road at 170 mph...

At least the officials took the correct line and Berger received a one-race ban, suspended for three races. Not that it did me much good as I kissed goodbye to the three points which would have moved me from tenth to equal eighth in the Championship.

I was really disappointed to have signed off the year on a low note, but the good thing was that by finishing second, Michael scored enough points to move into third place in the 1996 World Drivers' Championship and place Ferrari second in the Constructors' Championship. That was an excellent result for the team after such a difficult season. So, too, was Damon Hill's achievement in winning the race and the Championship.

I was really pleased for Damon. He had been in a horrible situation before the start of the race. Villeneuve could only win the Championship and Hill could only lose it. I would not have wanted to be in Damon's shoes. He made a good start and, even though his car was massively superior to everyone else's, he did the job despite having a lot of pressure on him. It would have been very sad if Damon had not won the Championship. Villeneuve has time on his side. Damon is older and, to be perfectly, honest, I don't think he's going to get another chance to take the title.

TWR Arrows will be good, but I don't think the team will reach the front. The top teams are too firmly established to allow a small team to win through, no matter how well organised they may be. Nonetheless, I think it is good for Formula 1 to have Stewart entering a team for 1997. I'm not a particularly great fan of Jackie Stewart but he will attract coverage because of who he is and he will do a proper job. We're not talking about Forti or some of the smaller teams who have been a joke in recent years.

The same applies to TWR Arrows. Tom Walkinshaw is a very shrewd guy. I had a deal with him to drive for Ligier in 1996 but the negotiations with Ferrari were happening at the same time. Tom was going to pay me good money and I have to admit I would like to drive for him at some time in the future. He's a tough nut but he is very committed to winning. He is not there for the money, he is there purely to win. The only team owners you can say that about in Formula 1 are Ron Dennis of McLaren and Frank Williams. Frank is ruthless in that respect.

At least I know that, despite our troubles, Ferrari are big enough and strong enough to become consistently successful. For me, this has been the worst year I have ever experienced in motor racing. But there is light at the end of the tunnel, and that's what it is all about. It is the difference between being stuck on a desert island, knowing there will never be any ships or planes passing by, and being marooned on an island where they come past from time to time. That's where you draw the line between hope and depression.

In fact, I have every hope of being a regular visitor to the podium in 1997. I really do believe Ferrari are going to get their act together. Yes, I know every team makes this claim at the end of a difficult season, but Ferrari will be the first to admit that there is room for improvement. Now almost all of the pieces are in place to make things better.

The new car is going to be a lot more competitive. Certainly, the latest engine is really nice to drive. I know and understand the team much better than before and I feel there will be a bit more effort channelled my way. The Championship may be a long way off from my point of view, but I am thinking seriously about a win next year as green races red to the top of the podium.

Formula 1 World Championship Results 1996

Round 1

Australian Grand Prix, Melbourne
10 March

58 laps of the 3.274-mile circuit

RESULTS

1	Damon Hill	Williams	58 laps
2	Jacques Villeneuve	Williams	58
3	**Eddie Irvine**	**Ferrari**	**58**
4	Gerhard Berger	Benetton	58
5	Mika Hakkinen	McLaren	58
6	Mika Salo	Tyrrell	57

WINNER'S FINISHING TIME
1hr 32m 50.491s; 123.494 mph

FASTEST LAP
Villeneuve, 1m 33.412s

POLE POSITION
Villeneuve, 1m 32.371s

The race is stopped and restarted after a first-lap multiple pile-up. Villeneuve leads until five laps from the end when an oil leak forces him to let Hill through, his Williams team-mate having run in close company for most of the race. Michael Schumacher holds third place before eventually retiring with brake trouble. Eddie Irvine assumes third and enjoys a lonely if trouble-free run during his first Grand Prix for Ferrari.

IRVINE'S COMMENT
'After all the troubles we'd had with the new car, I was as surprised as anyone when I finished third. Quite honestly, I didn't see it as a big deal. It wasn't one of the season's outstanding drives!'

Round 2

Brazilian Grand Prix, Interlagos, Sao Paulo
31 March

71 laps of the 2.687-mile circuit

RESULTS

1	Damon Hill	Williams	71 laps
2	Jean Alesi	Benetton	71
3	Michael Schumacher	Ferrari	70
4	Mika Hakkinen	McLaren	70
5	Mika Salo	Tyrrell	70
6	Olivier Panis	Ligier	70

WINNER'S FINISHING TIME
1hr 49m 52.976s; 104.19 mph

FASTEST LAP
Hill, 1m 21.547s

POLE POSITION
Hill, 1m 18.111s

Hill dominates a race which starts in pouring rain and finishes on a drying track. Villeneuve spins off, as does Barrichello after starting from the front row of the grid. Schumacher is lapped by Hill but finishes third. Irvine struggles with a misfire and poor handling to come home in seventh place.

IRVINE'S COMMENT
'After finishing third in Australia, I must admit I was a bit pissed off with seventh place...'

Round 3

Argentine Grand Prix, Buenos Aires
7 April

72 laps of the 2.646-mile circuit

RESULTS

1	Damon Hill	Williams	72 laps
2	Jacques Villeneuve	Williams	72
3	Jean Alesi	Benetton	72
4	Rubens Barrichello	Jordan	72
5	**Eddie Irvine**	**Ferrari**	**72**
6	Jos Verstappen	Arrows	72

WINNER'S FINISHING TIME
1hr 54m 55.322s; 99.43 mph

FASTEST LAP
Alesi, 1m 29.413s

POLE POSITION
Hill, 1m 30.346s

Three wins in succession for Hill, with Villeneuve giving Williams another one-two. Berger loses second place when the Benetton's suspension fails. A brilliant performance puts Schumacher on the front row but the Ferrari driver is forced to retire with handling problems. Irvine runs in the top 10 and struggles into fifth place with the Ferrari stuck in sixth gear.

IRVINE'S COMMENT
'I was really pleased to get two points out of an eventful race which hadn't promised much.'

Round 4

European Grand Prix, Nurburgring, Germany
28 April

67 laps of the 2.822-mile circuit

RESULTS

1	Jacques Villeneuve	Williams	67 laps
2	Michael Schumacher	Ferrari	67
3	David Coulthard	McLaren	67
4	Damon Hill	McLaren	67
5	Rubens Barrichello	Jordan	67
6	Martin Brundle	Jordan	67

WINNER'S FINISHING TIME
1hr 33m 26.473s; 120.03 mph

FASTEST LAP
Hill, 1m 21.363s

POLE POSITION
Hill, 1m 18.941s

A memorable race has Villeneuve calmly holding off an impressive Schumacher to score his first Grand Prix victory. Hill fluffs his start and has a miserable race, finishing fourth. Irvine is tapped into a spin by Panis on lap six but, by then, the Ferrari's race is already over thanks to a misfire.

IRVINE'S COMMENT
'A terrible start and then the misfire. Nothing more to say, really.'

Round 5

San Marino Grand Prix, Imola, Italy
5 May

63 laps of the 3.041-mile circuit

RESULTS

1	Damon Hill	Williams	63 laps
2	Michael Schumacher	Ferrari	63
3	Gerhard Berger	Benetton	63
4	**Eddie Irvine**	**Ferrari**	**63**
5	Rubens Barrichello	Jordan	63
6	Jean Alesi	Benetton	62

WINNER'S FINISHING TIME
1hr 35m 26.156s; 120.42 mph

FASTEST LAP
Hill, 1m 28.931s

POLE POSITION
Schumacher, 1m 26.890s

Hill regains control with a copybook win but Schumacher is the star of the weekend after taking pole position and finishing second. Villeneuve classified 11th after an early delay caused by a tangle with Alesi. After a poor start, Irvine finishes fourth.

IRVINE'S COMMENT
'After about five laps, I was in absolute agony.'

Round 6

Monaco Grand Prix, Monte Carlo
19 May

75 laps of the 2.06-mile circuit

RESULTS

1	Olivier Panis	Ligier	75 laps
2	David Coulthard	McLaren	75
3	Johnny Herbert	Sauber	75
4	Heinz-Harald Frentzen	Sauber	74
5	Mika Salo	Tyrrell	70
6	Mika Hakkinen	McLaren	70

WINNER'S FINISHING TIME
2hr 00m 45.692s; 77.06 mph

FASTEST LAP
Alesi, 1m 25.205s

POLE POSITION
Schumacher, 1m 20.356s

Another sensational pole position from Schumacher but an equally surprising mistake by the Ferrari driver on the first lap. Panis is the shock winner for Ligier, Irvine's eventful race ending in a spin and a collision.

IRVINE'S COMMENT
'I was classified seventh – a poor reward at the end of a race which had promised much.'

Round 7

Spanish Grand Prix, Barcelona
2 June

65 laps of the 2.93-mile circuit

RESULTS

1	Michael Schumacher	Ferrari	65 laps
2	Jean Alesi	Benetton	65
3	Jacques Villeneuve	Williams	65
4	Heinz-Harald Frentzen	Sauber	64
5	Mika Hakkinen	McLaren	64
6	Pedro Diniz	Ligier	63

WINNER'S FINISHING TIME
1hr 59m 49.307s; 95.56 mph

FASTEST LAP
Schumacher, 1m 45.517s

POLE POSITION
Hill, 1m 20.650s

A virtuoso performance by Schumacher in truly appalling conditions. Hill spins off and Villeneuve collects four points for an impressive third place. Irvine's race lasts for just one lap before spinning off.

IRVINE'S COMMENT
'The next thing I knew, I was spinning off the track...I don't know what caused it.'

Round 8

Canadian Grand Prix, Montreal
16 June

69 laps of the 2.74-mile circuit

RESULTS

1	Damon Hill	Williams	69 laps
2	Jacques Villeneuve	Williams	69
3	Jean Alesi	Benetton	69
4	David Coulthard	McLaren	69
5	Mika Hakkinen	McLaren	68
6	Martin Brundle	Jordan	68

WINNER'S FINISHING TIME
1hr 36m 03.465s; 118.40 mph

FASTEST LAP
Villeneuve, 1m 21.916s

POLE POSITION
Hill, 1m 21.059s

Hill controls the race from start to finish, beating Villeneuve at home. A terrible race for Ferrari: Schumacher starting from the back of the grid before retiring with broken transmission, Irvine going out with a broken suspension on lap 2.

IRVINE'S COMMENT
'I genuinely felt that this was going to be a good race for me...'

Round 9

French Grand Prix, Magny-Cours
30 June

72 laps of the 2.64-mile circuit

RESULTS

1	Damon Hill	Williams	72 laps
2	Jacques Villeneuve	Williams	72
3	Jean Alesi	Benetton	72
4	Gerhard Berger	Benetton	72
5	Mika Hakkinen	McLaren	72
6	David Coulthard	McLaren	71

WINNER'S FINISHING TIME
1hr 36m 28.795s; 118.17 mph

FASTEST LAP
Villeneuve, 1m 18.610s

POLE POSITION
Schumacher, 1m 15.989s

Yet another miserable Grand Prix for Ferrari. Schumacher's engine fails during the parade lap en route to the starting grid. Irvine, forced to start from the back of the grid because of a technical infringement, retires with gearbox trouble. Hill leads all the way.

IRVINE'S COMMENT
'The first time I'd ever started a race from the back of the grid and probably the first time two Ferraris have started from opposite ends, Michael on pole, me in last place. Or, at least we should have done, but Michael didn't get that far...'

Round 10

British Grand Prix, Silverstone
14 July

61 laps of the 3.152-mile circuit

RESULTS

1	Jacques Villeneuve	Williams	61 laps
2	Gerhard Berger	Benetton	61
3	Mika Hakkinen	McLaren	61
4	Rubens Barrichello	Jordan	61
5	David Coulthard	McLaren	60
6	Martin Brundle	Jordan	60

WINNER'S FINISHING TIME
1hr 33m 00.874s; 124.02 mph

FASTEST LAP
Villeneuve, 1m 29.288s

POLE POSITION
Hill, 1m 26.875s

Hill makes a bad start and struggles during his home Grand Prix until a mechanical failure spins him out, leaving team-mate Villeneuve to run unchallenged to his second win of the season. More early retirements for the Ferraris, Schumacher stopping on lap 4 with gearbox trouble, Irvine lasting for two more laps before engine failure brings more embarrassment.

IRVINE'S COMMENT
'I saw smoke coming from the back of Michael's car and I thought: "There'll be trouble over this...".'

Round 11

German Grand Prix, Hockenheim
28 July

45 laps of the 4.235-mile circuit

RESULTS

1	Damon Hill	Williams	45 laps
2	Jean Alesi	Benetton	45
3	Jacques Villeneuve	Williams	45
4	Michael Schumacher	Ferrari	45
5	David Coulthard	McLaren	45
6	Rubens Barrichello	Jordan	45

WINNER'S FINISHING TIME
1hr 21m 43.417s; 140.06 mph

FASTEST LAP
Hill, 1m 46.504s

POLE POSITION
Hill, 1m 43.912s

Hill takes his seventh win of the season after Berger's engine expires with three laps to run. Villeneuve moves into a distant third with Schumacher struggling into fourth place. Irvine runs with his team-mate before gearbox trouble brings another retirement.

IRVINE'S COMMENT
'Hardly a great race...'

197

Round 12

Hungarian Grand Prix, Hungaroring, Budapest
11 August

77 laps of the 2.465-mile circuit

RESULTS

1	Jacques Villeneuve	Williams	77 laps
2	Damon Hill	Williams	77
3	Jean Alesi	Benetton	77
4	Mika Hakkinen	McLaren	76
5	Olivier Panis	Ligier	76
6	Rubens Barrichello	Jordan	75

WINNER'S FINISHING TIME
1hr 46m 21.134s; 107.11 mph

FASTEST LAP
Hill, 1m 20.093s

POLE POSITION
Schumacher, 1m 17.129s

Another one-two for Williams, giving the British team the Constructors' Championship. Victory for Villeneuve cuts Hill's Championship lead to 17 points. Schumacher stays in contention until a late mechanical failure heralds another disappointing day for Ferrari, Irvine having lost sixth place with gearbox trouble.

IRVINE'S COMMENTS
'I was 1.4 seconds slower than Michael; the car was nowhere near what I wanted.'

Round 13

Belgian Grand Prix, Spa-Francorchamps
25 August

44 laps of the 4.33-mile circuit

RESULTS

1	Michael Schumacher	Ferrari	44 laps
2	Jacques Villeneuve	Williams	44
3	Mika Hakkinen	McLaren	44
4	Jean Alesi	Benetton	44
5	Damon Hill	Williams	44
6	Gerhard Berger	Benetton	44

WINNER'S FINISHING TIME
1hr 28m 15.125s; 129.52 mph

FASTEST LAP
Berger, 1m 53.067s

POLE POSITION
Villeneuve, 1m 50.574s

An exquisite performance from Schumacher and Ferrari as Williams run into trouble over tactics when the Safety Car is introduced. Yet another retirement for Irvine: gearbox again.

IRVINE'S COMMENT
'This retirement put me out of my misery. I was so far off the pace. The only good thing was that I was back in London before most people had left the circuit…'

Round 14

Italian Grand Prix, Monza
8 September

53 laps of the 3.604-mile circuit

RESULTS

1	Michael Schumacher	Ferrari	53 laps
2	Jean Alesi	Benetton	53
3	Mika Hakkinen	McLaren	53
4	Martin Brundle	Jordan	53
5	Rubens Barrichello	Jordan	53
6	Pedro Diniz	Ligier	52

WINNER'S FINISHING TIME
1hr 17m 43.632s; 146.67 mph

FASTEST LAP
Schumacher, 1m 26.110s

POLE POSITION
Hill, 1m 24.204s

Pandemonium as Schumacher wins for Ferrari and disappointment for Hill as he spins out of the lead while looking as if he could wrap up the championship. He is lucky, however, since Villeneuve also has trouble and finishes seventh. Irvine retires for the ninth race in succession – this time through driver error.

IRVINE'S COMMENTS
'I was completely gutted. To think, I could have been on the podium with Michael.'

Round 15

Portuguese Grand Prix, Estoril
22 September

70 laps of the 2.709-mile circuit

RESULTS

1	Jacques Villeneuve	Williams	70 laps
2	Damon Hill	Williams	70
3	Michael Schumacher	Ferrari	70
4	Jean Alesi	Benetton	70
5	**Eddie Irvine**	**Ferrari**	**70**
6	Gerhard Berger	Benetton	70

WINNER'S FINISHING TIME
1hr 40m 22.915s; 113.35 mph

FASTEST LAP
Villeneuve, 1m 22.873s

POLE POSITION
Hill, 1m 20.330s

A brilliant win for Villeneuve keeps the championship open as Hill finishes second. Schumacher takes third and Irvine enjoys a lively scrap with Berger to finish fifth.

IRVINE'S COMMENT
'It was great to score some points at long last! I had a good duel with Berger: no way he was going to take fifth place away from me.'

Round 16

Japanese Grand Prix, Suzuka
13 October

52 laps of the 3.644-mile circuit

RESULTS

1	Damon Hill	Williams	52 laps
2	Michael Schumacher	Ferrari	52
3	Mika Hakkinen	McLaren	52
4	Gerhard Berger	Benetton	52
5	Martin Brundle	Jordan	52
6	Heinz-Harald Frentzen	Sauber	52

WINNER'S FINISHING TIME
1hr 32m 33.791s; 122.73 mph

FASTEST LAP
Jacques Villeneuve, Williams, 1m 44.043s

POLE POSITION
Villeneuve, 1m 38.909s

Damon Hill became 1996 World Champion in the best possible way by leading the race from start to finish. Jacques Villeneuve made a bad start from pole position and retired from fourth place when a rear wheel came off. Second place for Michael Schumacher gave him third place in the driver's championship. Eddie Irvine, bundled out of fourth place by Berger's Benetton.

IRVINE'S COMMENT
'I was bloody annoyed. Fourth place would have been a nice way to end the season. This was the second race in succession where Berger had driven into me. I said once, fair enough. But twice! That's ridiculous!'

Final Championship Positions

DRIVERS

1	Damon Hill	97 points
2	Jacques Villeneuve	78
3	Michael Schumacher	59
4	Jean Alesi	47
5	Mika Hakkinen	31
6	Gerhard Berger	21
7	David Coulthard	18
8	Rubens Barrichello	14
9	Olivier Panis	13
10	Eddie Irvine	11
11	Martin Brundle	8
12	Heinz-Harald Frentzen	7
13	Mika Salo	5
14	Johnny Herbert	4
15	Pedro Diniz	2
16	Jos Verstappen	1

TEAMS

1	Williams	175 points
2	Ferrari	70
3	Benetton	68
4	McLaren	49
5	Jordan	22
6	Ligier	15
7	Sauber	11
8	Tyrrell	5
9	Footwork	1

NUMBER OF WINS

Damon Hill	8
Jacques Villeneuve	4
Michael Schumacher	3
Olivier Panis	1
Williams	12
Ferrari	3
Ligier	1

POLE POSITIONS

Damon Hill	9
Michael Schumacher	4
Jacques Villeneuve	3

FASTEST LAPS

Jacques Villeneuve	6
Damon Hill	5
Michael Schumacher	2
Jean Alesi	2
Gerhard Berger	1

EDDIE IRVINE

Best result: 3rd. Australian Grand Prix
Best grid position: 3rd. Australian Grand Prix

Eddie Irvine

1965	10 November. Born Newtownards, Northern Ireland
1983	Motor racing debut. Formula Ford
1984–86	Private entrant in Irish Formula Ford series
1987	Works Van Dieman Formula Ford drive RAC Formula Ford Champion Esso Formula Ford Champion
1988	British Formula 3 Championship
1989	International Formula 3000 Championship
1990	3rd: International Formula 3000 Championship
1991	7th: Japanese Formula 3000 Championship
1992	8th: Japanese Formula 3000 Championship
1993	2nd: Japanese Formula 3000 Championship Lap record and 4th at Le Mans Grand Prix debut in Japan with Jordan
1994	16th: Formula 1 World Championship with Jordan 2nd: Le Mans
1995	12th: Formula 1 World Championship with Jordan
1996	10th: Formula 1 World Championship with Ferrari

Index

Guam, holiday 128

Hakkinen, Mika 43, 101–2, 116
  Argentinian Grand Prix 1996 53
  Irvine's assessment of 170
Hamilton, Maurice 9
Herbert, Johnny 108
  Australian Grand Prix 1996 28
  Italian Grand Prix 1994 142
Hicks, Tom 158
Higgins, Derek 65
Hill, Damon 69, 87, 95, 97
  Adelaide Grand Prix 1994 167
  Argentinian Grand Prix 1996 51, 52
  Australian Grand Prix 1996 27, 29, 30
  Brazilian Grand Prix 1996 44
  Canadian Grand Prix 1996 117
  Hungarian Grand Prix 1996 146
  Irvine's assessment of 168–70
  Italian Grand Prix 1996 161
  Japanese Grand Prix 1993 12, 135, 136
  Japanese Grand Prix 1996 202
  Portuguese Grand Prix 1996 166
  Spanish Grand Prix 1996 113
  Williams, departure from 153, 155–6, 157, 169
Hockenheim see German Grand Prix
Hungarian Grand Prix 1996 146–7, 198
Hungaroring see Hungarian Grand Prix
Hunt, James 73, 75–6, 78
hydraulics, gearbox 121

Imola see San Marino Grand Prix
Indycar racing 70, 85
Interlagos see Brazilian Grand Prix
Ireland, background 36–9
Irvine, Eddie
  back problems 85–6, 88, 116

best results 206
childhood 47–8, 73
chronology 209
concentration 163
Dublin house 40
fashion shoot 92
father 47, 80, 133
fitness 73, 138–9
flying lessons 111–12
Formula 1 debut 133–6
helicopter licence 145–6
helmet colours 38–9
house 159
Ireland problems 37–9
Japan 81–2, 106–9
jet-ski 145
mother 133
nationality question 36–7
private jet 157, 158–9
Schumacher 71
Senna incident 13, 136–7, 140, 142
sister 9, 172
sponsorship need 79–80
taxi company 159
tennis 159–60
Irvine, Edmund (father) 47, 80, 133
Irvine, Sonia (sister) 9, 172
Italian Grand Prix 1990 80
Italian Grand Prix 1994 142–3
Italian Grand Prix 1996 67–8, 155, 160–3, 200
pre-race tests 157

Japan
  Fuji Formula 3 circuit 106
  Krosnoff 128
  Senna 177
  sportscar racing 81
Japanese Grand Prix 1989 167
Japanese Grand Prix 1993 12–13, 106, 108, 134–6, 140
Japanese Grand Prix 1996

Acknowledgements

When I set out to write this book with Eddie, two things were clear in my mind. His career had turned the final corner and I felt sure podium finishes would be a regular occurrence. Indeed, he might even sneak the odd win. With Irvine, anything seemed possible and racing for Ferrari would do justice to a huge natural talent.

But I approached the task with some trepidation. I was certain that Eddie had no idea about the amount of work involved. His disregard for convention promised a difficult season as I attempted to extract the commitment and time necessary for taping and reading of proofs. The glory was certain. The telling of it would be the difficult part.

I was wrong on both counts. The 1996 Formula 1 season has been the worst Irvine has ever experienced in terms of results. The frustration generated by nine retirements in succession has had no equal in his thirteen years of racing. And yet he has been the model of professionalism, both in and out of the cockpit. Always willing to talk, it was Eddie who chased me; his enthusiasm for the project never wavered. Far from being a record of success, the story has been one of fortitude, honesty and good humour. If anything, the book is the stronger for it.

For those who judge drivers purely on hard results, Irvine has been an easy target to write off. But more seasoned observers have realised the true value of this character-forming season, the intimate details of which have been revealed within these pages. Perhaps no one is more aware of Eddie's plight than his Ferrari team-mate, Michael Schumacher.

'He has had a difficult year,' said Schumacher. 'For sure, there were certain races where he was not able to get the same quality of car that I had because we were short of parts and it is normal that whichever driver is quicker, he will get them first. But it's very rare to find a team-mate who will accept that and be able to withstand all the bad luck and problems he has had this year. Not finishing so many races and still being in the mood he is in and still being positive... I have known other team-mates who become negative and start to criticise and so on. I have to say, he has done pretty well. With all the team-mates I have had, and considering the difficult circumstances, in my view he is the best I have worked with.'

Schumacher's views are endorsed by Jackie Stewart, the three-times World Champion making this observation: 'Being number two to the best driver in the world is always a thankless task, but I think Eddie Irvine has dealt with it very well. In a way, he's well suited to the role. He's got that air of acceptance about him yet he still looks comfortable and relaxed. I'm sure there must be moments when that's not the case, but he carries himself well.'

You can make your own judgement after reading this book.

I must thank several people for their assistance: Giancarlo Baccini, Edmund and Kathleen Irvine, Sonia Irvine, Rod Vickery, Michael Doggart and Tom Whiting of publishers HarperCollins, Gerald Donaldson as we compared notes while writing similar books, Di Wakefield and my wife Diane for help in transcribing the tapes and, last but not least, the man himself. Thanks, Eddie. It's been great crack.

Maurice Hamilton